Never Mind the Bullocks

A Twenty-First Century Exploration of the Torah
for *bar-/bat-mitzvah Students*

(*or anyone who wants to know why Jewish people celebrate turning 13 by reading Hebrew)

Rabbi Pete Tobias

authorHOUSE®

Also by the same author:
'Liberal Judaism: A Judaism for the Twenty-First Century (2007)

This book is dedicated to all the Jewish summer camps
that I have encountered and enjoyed
and, in particular, to my memories of
ULPS Kadimah Summer School,
where I learned more about bullocks
than anywhere else in my life,
and to
Rabbi Andrew Goldstein
who helped me understand their – and my – place in Judaism.

PT September 2008/*Elul 5768*

AuthorHouse™ UK Ltd.
500 Avebury Boulevard
Central Milton Keynes, MK9 2BE
www.authorhouse.co.uk
Phone: 08001974150

First published by AuthorHouse 1/23/2009

ISBN: 978-1-4389-2529-5 (sc)

The production of this book was funded by the NLPS Trust for Progressive Judasim

Printed in the United States of America
Bloomington, Indiana

This book is printed on acid-free paper.

Table of Contents

Prologue: First Encounter   1

Lesson One   8

Second Encounter   12

Lesson Two   16

Third Encounter   22

Lesson Three   26

Fourth Encounter   32

Lesson Four   36

Fifth Encounter   43

Lesson Five   47

Tish'ah b'Av   54

Sixth Encounter   59

Lesson Six   63

Seventh Encounter   69

Lesson Seven   73

Eighth Encounter   81

Lesson Eight   85

Ninth Encounter   92

Lesson Nine   96

Final Encounter   103

Lesson Ten   107

Monday Night   113

Lesson Eleven   117

Epilogue   125

The Lesson Plans   127

Suggested Further Reading   156

ABOUT THIS BOOK

The purpose of this book is to encourage those who read it to think about the origins of the Torah and the possible intentions of those who wrote and compiled it. As such, it is mainly – though by no means exclusively – intended for those approaching the ceremony of bar- or bat-mitzvah – whether they be parents or teachers of twelve-year-old children or the children themselves.

It can be used in a variety of ways. It is primarily a teaching course and plans for the eleven individual lessons are at the end of the book. The content of these lessons is somewhat unconventional, so a significant section of the book is a fictionalised account of the lessons actually being taught to a group of twelve-year-old children in a Californian Jewish summer camp. Apart from the teacher, however, all the characters are fictitious as are the incidents in the story and, indeed, the camp itself. The 'lessons' can, if desired, be read aloud with a bar-/bat-mitzvah group as a means of teaching the course – discussions can always follow afterwards. The chapters containing the lessons can be read as a complete unit: they stand alone as a challenging critique of the origins and purpose of the Torah suitable for younger readers.

Each lesson is preceded by a 'conversation' between the author/teacher and a manifestation of the biblical prophet Isaiah. It is for the reader to decide whether or not these 'conversations' are actually taking place or if they are a figment of the author's imagination. Their purpose is to provide background material to the forthcoming lesson and, as such, they provide a useful introduction for the teacher planning the lessons for a class. They also offer hints at what the author believes to be a plausible explanation of the origins of the Torah for which significant scholarly support can be found. As such, it is also a work that should be of interest to anyone considering the origins of the Five Books of Moses and looking for an understanding of the differences between the Liberal and Orthodox approaches to that document.

The Torah is an ancient text from which Jewish children read at a key stage of their religious development. For too many, however, the ceremony of bar-/bat-mitzvah effectively signals an end to their engagement with their religious heritage. Perhaps more than anything else, this book is an attempt to provide the puzzled twelve-year-old that lurks somewhere inside all Jews who found themselves preparing to read from this extraordinary book with answers to questions they weren't allowed to ask. If Judaism felt like a series of peculiar customs and practices to be carried out without challenge in the name of 'tradition', if those Bible stories we learned at cheder, or revisited every Passover always seemed just a little far-fetched, if religion seemed to be irrelevant to and have nothing to say about our modern world – or if that's still the case – then hopefully this book will encourage readers to do what, for the most part, as twelve-year-olds, we weren't expected to do: think again.

Rabbi Pete Tobias
September 2008

PROLOGUE

The first encounter – Saturday morning

The moment had arrived. In I strode, the white sheet that I had purchased the day before from the local Wal-Mart sweeping majestically behind me – or so I imagined. There were about fifty children, ten or eleven years old, plus some twenty or so adults – mostly camp counsellors in their late teens plus a few more senior staff members. Seated on three sides of a sort of arena with banked steps wide enough to sit on, they all watched as I stormed into the middle of this arena, wagging the forefinger of my right hand at them, simulating furious indignation as I yelled.

'Well, what do you think you're doing?' I paused to survey them. 'Who asked you to sit around and recite all these words and sing all these songs? Are you listening to the words you recite? Do you understand the meaning of your prayers? And who are you praying to?'

I looked around at the faces all watching me, seeing amusement and bemusement in roughly equal measure. I strode purposefully – menacingly even – towards a group in the corner.

'This is what God is saying to you,' I bellowed. 'I have had enough of your singing and your prayers. When you pray to Me, I will hide My eyes from you. I shall not listen to you. Because you do not listen to Me –'

I wheeled away from the corner of the arena and pointed to a table which was the focal point of this gathering. There was a rabbi standing behind it, a woman, wearing a brightly coloured prayer shawl and large, matching skullcap. In front of her was a Torah from which she had just been reading as part of this Shabbat morning service.

'– and you do not listen to My words,' I continued. I marched to the table and picked up the scroll, which had been wrapped in its decorative cover following the reading. I tucked it gently – lovingly almost – under my left arm, resting against my shoulder and turned to face the bewildered audience for one last time. 'This Torah is to teach you how to live your lives and do God's will,' I said slowly. 'To do justice and deal kindly with one another. Learn to do good!'

I turned and swept out of the arena, scroll nestling under my chin. As I left, I winked at the rabbi, as if to say, 'See if you can explain what that was all about!' She stared blankly back at me, and it was as I was climbing up the grassy bank to my next destination that I realised that she wouldn't have been able to see my winking eye. It was covered by a piece of card that I had attached to the right lens of my clip-on sunglasses. This piece of card protruded above the frame of my sunglasses and there was a rather crude attempt at a human eye drawn in the upper half of it, making it appear that my eyes were not level. This cardboard 'eye' covered the right side of my forehead and collided with the rim of my very English sunhat as I strode up the hill, hoping to arrive in good time for my next performance.

As I reached the tree just behind the venue known as the auditorium, I could hear the congregation at prayer in it were in the middle of the *Amidah*. That meant I had a few minutes to spare. I sat back against the tree and surveyed the beautiful Californian landscape – the green slopes topped with pine trees set against a background of an impossibly blue sky. At the bottom of the hill I could see the building that housed the large dining hall and the various administrative offices of the summer camp. There was a rare and awesome peace that Saturday morning – in various locations around the sprawling site of this residential camp, several groups of young people were engaged in Sabbath worship. The fact that there were more groups praying than there were scrolls to read from meant that the services were staggered and I had been given the responsibility of delivering the scroll I was holding from one venue to another. It was a role I enjoyed, since on this particular Shabbat, it had given me a unique opportunity to deliver the words of the *haftarah*, words of the prophet Isaiah that were traditionally read on the Shabbat before *Tish'ah b'Av* – the ninth of Av – anniversary of the destruction of the First and Second Temples in Jerusalem by the Babylonians and the Romans in 586 BCE and 70 CE respectively.

I recalled with amusement the conversation I had shared with my American rabbinic colleagues who were part of the faculty at the summer camp when we had discussed these Shabbat services a couple of days ago. They were already intrigued at the presence of a middle-aged English rabbi in their midst; my wish to dress up as the prophet Isaiah seemed only to add to their perception that all English people were eccentric. The difference between the English and American pronunciation of his name didn't help either. I had already upset them when I had questioned the need to conduct lunchtime Hebrew lessons with those twelve-year-old campers whose parents had insisted that they continue to prepare for their *bar-* and *bat-mitzvah* ceremonies, even though this was supposed to be a vacation. It was made clear to me that we had a duty to honour the wishes of those parents. So for the last three days I had dutifully sat under this very tree with three unhappy campers - Josh, Darren and Jess – and listened to them take it in turns to struggle through their Torah portions. And as I waited for my moment to enter the auditorium where those three sat along with seventy or so of their peers, I also recalled my

own *bar-mitzvah* ceremony. It had taken place in an Orthodox English synagogue and I had dutifully chanted several verses from the Torah and even more from the book purportedly written by the person whom I was trying to impersonate that Saturday morning.

'Who are you supposed to be?' This question, hissed from somewhere above or behind me, interrupted my train of thought. Puzzled, I cast curious, one-eyed glances all around me but could see nothing except the tree against which I was leaning. 'And what is that you are holding?' There it was again – it sounded as though the voice was coming from inside the tree. Carefully clutching the Torah, I stood up, almost tripping myself by standing on my Wal-Mart sheet. I turned to look up at the tree, momentarily struggling to keep my balance.

Against my better judgment, I decided to speak. 'Who's there?' I whispered, rather hoping that I wouldn't actually be heard.

'My name is *Yeshayahu ben Amoz*.' I looked nervously around, turning my head awkwardly on account of one eye being covered – more worried that someone might see me having a conversation with a tree that claimed to be or to contain Isaiah the Prophet than at the thought that this was really happening to me. There was no one else nearby, and the only sound was that of the nearby twelve-year-olds singing words from the book of Exodus that celebrated the Sabbath, accompanied by guitars.

Cautiously, I lowered myself to the ground once again, and rested the Torah in my lap.

'I have answered your question,' said the voice. 'Now you must answer mine.'

'Which one?' I retorted, still struggling to believe that I was having a conversation with a tree.

'Let's start with what you are holding,' replied the voice. 'It seems more interesting than the ridiculous costume you are wearing.'

'It's a scroll,' I sighed.

'Is that the document to which you have been referring when you have studied here with some children?' he asked. 'I have heard them reading in the Hebrew tongue – slowly and painfully, if I may say so. What is the purpose of this exercise?'

Looking back on that incident now, I have a sense of acute embarrassment at the absurdity of the scene. There I was, halfway up a grassy slope, wrapped in a white sheet, clutching a Torah, with a peculiar cardboard eye attached to the right lens of my sunglasses, explaining to a tree the nature of a twenty-first century *bar-* or *bat-mitzvah* ceremony.

Nevertheless, I was pleased to have the opportunity to put into words the thoughts that had been going through my mind at the moment our 'conversation' had begun. As I explained the requirement for a child turning thirteen to go through a kind of ordeal by reading words in a foreign language from an ancient text, I was struck by the absurdity of this rite of passage that purported to represent some kind of entry into Jewish adulthood. When the Rabbis of two thousand years earlier had decreed that boys became men at the age of thirteen, their intention had been that from that age onwards, the young men should take responsibility for actually carrying out the obligations of Judaism rather than simply learning about them.

'But now a *bar-* or *bat-mitzvah* ceremony seems to be the end of a child's involvement with Judaism,' I said aloud, surprised at the indignation in my voice. 'And the whole process of Jewish education seems to be geared to this brief synagogue performance rather than seeking to explain what Judaism is about and why this -' I indicated the Torah that I was clutching, 'is so central to our heritage.'

'You still have not explained to me what it is,' said the voice from above and behind me. I was momentarily taken aback at the fact that Isaiah did not recognise the Torah. A quick calculation revealed that if, as modern scholarship would have us believe, it was written or compiled just before or during the Babylonian exile in the sixth century BCE, then Isaiah would have lived some two hundred years before it came into being. The fact that Isaiah didn't know what the Torah was proved that what I'd been told as I prepared for my *bar-mitzvah* ceremony – namely that it had all been written or dictated by God to Moses – wasn't true, since Moses had lived at least half a millennium earlier.

'It's called the Torah,' I said, vaguely amused to be explaining this to a prophet from the eighth century BCE. I was about to offer an outline of its contents when the voice offered a rather cryptic reply.

'That was the project we started in Jerusalem!' he exclaimed. I listened as he told me of a school of prophets and teachers in his day who were dismayed by the level of corruption and lack of justice in the kingdoms of Judah and Israel.

'We gave speeches and made proclamations, imploring the people to listen to the God of Israel who demanded justice,' he continued. I closed my eyes and could picture men like Amos, Isaiah and Micah whose teachings are at the heart of Liberal Judaism, shouting at the worshippers of Judah and Israel, insisting that they protect the vulnerable members of their society and warning them of God's anger if they did not.

The voice told me of visions and sayings that were recorded on clay tablets and parchment scrolls, political commentaries and historical accounts of kings who led their people astray or sought to guide them on a path of righteousness, of attacks on corrupt priests leading the people in meaningless sacrifices, and the casual cruelty of the wealthy towards the poor and dispossessed.

'And we saw how this corruption, this emptiness would bring destruction on the people,' said the voice, in a whisper that sounded as though it was inside my head rather than from somewhere beyond me. 'So we warned of the danger and we begged that they change their ways in order to avert the catastrophe that threatened, but it was to no avail. The kingdom of Israel was destroyed by the Assyrians, who then marched to the very gates of Jerusalem.' There was a pause, as though a painful memory was being recalled.

'But the armies withdrew after King Ahaz swore loyalty to the Assyrian emperor Sennacherib – against my advice. Jerusalem was saved but the lesson had to be learned. So our project to create the Torah of *YHWH*[1] – the teaching of the Eternal One – began. There were teachings and instructions brought by the men of Shiloh who fled the destruction of Israel. We learned from their wisdom and added our own insights, determined to ensure that the people of Judah mended their ways and did not suffer the same fate as their northern cousins –'

'But they did,' I said softly. 'Which is why we read your words of warning on this Shabbat, the one that precedes the anniversary of the destruction of Jerusalem and its Temple just over a hundred years after you lived.'

'So our teachings were not heeded,' he said sadly. I shook my head.

'But they were remembered,' I replied, gently patting the scroll that nestled in my lap. 'Perhaps this is the result of the project you started. Reminding us of what this religion, this life is supposed to be about.'

'And how is this teaching used in your day?'

I explained how the Torah was divided up into fifty-four sections and that during the course of a year in Orthodox synagogues, the entire Torah would be chanted in Hebrew. I explained how Liberal and Reform Jews only heard a short section of each week's

---

[1] *YHWH*, the four Hebrew letters used to denote the name of Israel's God. The actual pronunciation of this name is unknown; it is assumed to be *Yahweh* but as it is regarded as a holy name, it is pronounced in modern-day Jewish circles as *Adonai*. See p.103ff.

portion, and was prepared to defend this policy on the grounds that this weekly excerpt was accompanied by translation and explanation, but no challenge came.

'And the wisdom of each generation has been added to this Torah?' he inquired. I laughed.

'No way! About six centuries after you lived, the whole thing was deemed to have been written by God. Nothing has been added or taken away and in Orthodox circles every word is regarded as representing divinely revealed truth.'

I imagined I heard the branches of the tree shaking, as though he were expressing amusement or indignation, or both.

'Words written two and a half thousand years ago in a time and a place so removed and distant from here?' he exclaimed. 'Socially and politically, culturally and economically – how can the situations on which our words were based possibly have meaning and relevance to you? You said earlier that the Temple was destroyed, and with no Temple, there can be no sacrifices, no priests. Unless the Temple stands again ...?'

'It did, but was destroyed for a second time almost two thousand years ago. Those who believe in the divine authorship of this document believe that it will be rebuilt a third time – and that sacrifice should once again be offered.'

'Why would a return to sacrifice be necessary?' he asked. 'It is clear that you have evolved different ways of communicating with God.' He paused and the sound of guitar chords to accompany words from Psalm 19 – 'May the words of our mouths and the meditations of our hearts be acceptable to You, O God, our Rock and our Redeemer' filled the air.

'The purpose of such offerings is unchanged, he continued, 'but the manner in which they find expression cannot remain the same. Even in my day, it was clear that sacrificial worship was misunderstood and abused.'

'That's what I just told everyone!' I laughed. 'I used your words – declaring how God is weary of the offerings of rams and bullocks.' The reminder of the morning's *haftarah* suddenly alerted me to my role. It would soon be time for me to storm into the auditorium from which the singing was emerging, to deliver the Torah and the vision of the prophet Isaiah, condemning worship without sincerity, attacking empty words of prayer that do not inspire the worshippers to seek and implement in their society the justice that God demanded.

'The world has changed since my day,' he continued. 'How then can those who are the inheritors of my tradition, my faith, my work still cling to stories and regulations that belong to another time, another place?'

'But surely the messages you taught can be applied to all lands and ages?' I protested.

'You are right,' he agreed. 'But we presented them in a way that would speak to the people living in that time and in that place. They were encouraged to think about their lives, their world, their relationship with God in terms that they would understand. Twelve-year-old children in a sophisticated society more than two thousand years later cannot be taught by those same examples. Would I be correct in saying that most of your students find this Torah confusing, outdated and irrelevant?'

I nodded. 'This is hardly surprising,' he went on. 'All the talk of priests and the sacrifice of rams and bullocks cannot have any meaning for them.' There was a pause, during which the guitar-accompanied singing from below where I sat came to an end.

'I need to go,' I said, and began to pick myself up, leaning on the tree to ensure that I carried the scroll safely.

'I think I begin to understand why I am here,' said the voice from the tree as I prepared to move away. Suddenly the absurdity of the situation was brought back to me and I looked around to make sure that no one else was witnessing an English rabbi in his mid-forties engaged in conversation with a tree.

'The lunchtime lessons with your *bar-* and *bat-mitzvah* students that take place here,' he said. 'They are an opportunity to instruct these children of the true purpose of the document from which they will read. You must encourage them to explore its origins, the history that led to it being written, and to seek to comprehend what motivated me and those like me to compile it. They must understand that to follow it blindly and to accept every word as being divine truth is as empty as the offerings of rams and bullocks against which I railed in the Temple forecourt all those years ago...' His voice trailed off, as though wistfully recalling that distant episode.

'We must teach people what is the true purpose of this religious heritage,' he went on, determination in his voice. 'That religion is not about empty offerings and hollow words of praise. That it is meant to be understood and learned from, not elevated and revered. It comes from our people's hearts and should awaken our people's hearts to the truth of this world, our world. We must lead these people away from this ceremony, this singing, this praying. We must move them from their empty words and hollow prayers, turn their hearts to God's true purpose and −'

'And never mind the bullocks,' I interjected.

'Well yes,' he said, sounding put out at being interrupted in full flow. 'True religion is not about sacrificing bullocks, it is about encouraging people to find meaning in our world.'

'And that is what I am called upon to do right now,' I exclaimed, marching off down the hillside towards the auditorium. It was only as I was on my way there, that I wondered how a prophet from the eighth century BCE managed to understand and speak English. But that, and the general insanity of a conversation with a tree, was forgotten as I once again launched into my Isaiah speech, hurling pseudo-prophetic wrath at a bunch of uninterested twelve and thirteen year-old American Jews preparing to hear the Torah being read beneath the bright California sunshine.

'This is what God says to you,' I bellowed …

* * * * * * * * * * * *

After the morning's services had ended, I returned to my cabin and removed the now grubby sheet and one-eyed, clip-on sunglasses that purported to transform me into the ancient prophet Isaiah. I thought back to the extraordinary encounter that had taken place between my appearances in the services, the questions about the origins and the purpose of the Torah, this document from which Jewish children read a short excerpt as some kind of transition into adulthood. Had I really just had a conversation with a tree that somehow contained the biblical prophet whom I had impersonated that Saturday morning in California? Or had the fact that I was dressed as him and proclaimed some of his words given me a mysterious insight into what motivated and inspired him?

Whatever it was, the incident had certainly motivated and inspired me. I realised that preparation for a *bar-* or *bat-mitzvah* ceremony wasn't just about learning to read out a few words in a foreign language, though that was all it seemed to have become – plus a party and a whole load of gifts, of course. But now I proposed to dispense with the dull routine of listening to my three students take it in turns to read their blessings and sections from their Torah portions. That's how it had been for the three days since camp had begun – and we were all thoroughly fed up with it. I recalled our first meeting: to them I was just some rabbi with a strange accent ('are you Australian?') and to me they were three kids at camp called Darren, Jess and Josh, whom I was apparently meant to help with their Hebrew reading. After my Saturday morning experience I decided I was no longer going to spend every lunchtime ploughing painfully through a few Hebrew words with these kids. Those skills could be learned elsewhere – I wanted to give them a sense of what this document was and why they were reading from it.

One of the most important reasons for reading from the Torah and celebrating a *bar-* or *bat-mitzvah* ceremony was the connection with a tradition stretching back for generations. I needed something that could provoke their interest more than just talking to them, though if all else failed, I figured I could do that too. Then I remembered that somewhere in my laptop computer was an episode of the TV comedy 'The Wonder Years' dealing with a *bar-mitzvah* ceremony. I could show this to my students as an introduction to my attempt to teach them a new perspective on the Torah between now and when they finished at camp in ten days' time.

Once I found the episode, I realised that it would probably be a good idea to think through what I wanted to teach and how I planned to present it. It was a tradition of the summer camp that all educational programmes – they called them by the Hebrew name of *tochniot* (singular *tochnit*) – had to be structured. There were the Aims, the broad concepts that it was hoped would be put across during the course of the *tochnit*. Then there were the Objectives – more specific goals that a child (referred to by the Hebrew name of *chanich*, plural *chanichim*) would be able to demonstrate once the lesson was over. In order to conceptualise this properly, Objectives were preceded by the rather frightening acronym ATEOTTCWBAT, which stood for At The End Of This *Tochnit Chanichim* Will Be Able To … followed by whatever it was they would be able to do. So the Objectives had to complete the sentence beginning with those words. Sometimes that was hard because you could never say for sure that a student would be able to know or understand something, so there were phrases like 'articulate an awareness of …' or 'demonstrate knowledge of …' trying to define what could actually be deemed to have been learned in any educational environment.

So I typed up and printed out the first lesson plan for my new look *bar-* and *bat-mitzvah* class, based on the reflections that had taken place under the tree at the location where those lessons would be given. I packed the laptop into a bag and headed off to the dining hall, wondering how my three students would respond to this new approach to preparation for their *bar-* and *bat-mitzvah* ceremonies.

* * * * * * * * * * * * *

LESSON ONE – Saturday afternoon

'So what's a *bar-mitzvah* anyway?'

My three students were a little puzzled when they were told not to bother opening their plastic see-through folders that contained the copies of their portions and their CDs, but the opportunity to watch a TV programme seemed to please them. They arranged themselves in order to be able to see the small screen and hear the dialogue of the TV programme I hoped would get them thinking about the significance of the ceremony for which they were preparing.

The programme was one episode of a long-running series based on the story of Kevin Arnold growing up in 1960's America. His best friend, Paul, with whom he had shared his life from an early age, was Jewish and Kevin was not. The first – and perhaps only – time that this had an impact on their relationship was when they turned thirteen and Paul's *bar-mitzvah* ceremony, which took place on the day of Kevin's thirteenth birthday, highlighted a number of cultural differences. In particular, it showed that Paul had a very strong identity and a sense of continuity within the Jewish community whereas the mixture of roots in Kevin's family left him somewhat adrift. Following the Friday night dinner scene, at which Paul's grandfather emphasises the significance of the *bar-mitzvah* ceremony, Kevin asks his mother 'what are we?' He receives an answer that combines Poland, Scandinavia and New Jersey and leads him to conclude that he is, like most Americans, 'a mutt'.

I noticed that the students were watching the DVD with varying degrees of disinterest – my students would much rather have been with their friends in their cabins talking about whatever Californian twelve-year-olds talk about. But there were some things that they could identify with – I saw it, even though they were trying hard not to betray it. Like the scene on the school bus at the beginning when Kevin's older brother is taunting Paul, a speech that begins with the words 'so what's a *bar-mitzvah* anyway?' And of course the bit that most impresses his non-Jewish audience on the bus is the mention of the presents and the money he anticipates receiving for this event.

That was also the part that seemed to occupy the minds of those who had reluctantly viewed the DVD. If my intention had been to impress upon my young audience the deeper significance of the life-cycle event for which they were studying and move them beyond its materialistic rewards, then it seemed to have failed quite dismally.

'A thousand bucks was all he was going to get for his *bar-mitzvah*?' That was the first comment after I opened the discussion. It came from Josh, who was almost prone on the ground, only the peak of his LA Dodgers baseball cap (which was pointing backwards, of course) prevented him from lying completely flat on the ground. Jess and Darren laughed.

I was annoyed but determined not to show it. 'So is that all this *bar-/bat-mitzvah* thing means to you guys?' I asked. I suppose I deserved the answer I got.

'You want us to say how important it is for us to take our place as adults in the Jewish community, right?' Darren was smiling as he asked the question and when I looked into his blue eyes, I saw no malice in them. His smile was bright and genuine, and, unusually, his teeth were not wrapped in the metal bands that seemed to be an obligatory part of Californian teenage appearance, like some kind of fashion statement. He had a long face with thin protruding cheekbones and a slightly off-centre nose that made him look as though he had been beaten in a fight – and had there been such a fight, his slight, almost fragile physique would have guaranteed defeat.

'Well what do you think it's for, then?' I replied, still trying not to get irritated. It was a conversation I'd had with so many Jewish twelve-year-olds before. They either said how much they were looking forward to the presents and the party or trotted out some insincere rubbish about becoming an adult.

'Even the kid in the movie said it was about becoming a man,' was Darren's response.

'So how does that make you feel, Jess?' I felt it was important to get the only girl in the trio involved in this male-oriented *bar-mitzvah* conversation.

'Well, the presents and the party are going to be awesome!' she exclaimed. The sunlight made the glitter on her eyelids and the metal on her teeth glisten – with her too-perfectly trimmed shoulder-length blonde hair and symmetrical facial features, her appearance was frighteningly close to the cliché of the Jewish American Princess.

'But what about you becoming a man?' I insisted, which got a grudging laugh from all three of them. 'I mean - how many of your girlfriends are having a *bat-mitzvah* ceremony too?'

'Maybe two or three,' she replied, sitting upright and folding her arms as though about to make a serious point. 'I do get a bit annoyed when people always talk about *bar-mitzvah* though – like as if what girls do isn't so important.'

'It isn't!' exclaimed Josh, and rolled over to avoid the not entirely playful blow that Jess aimed at him. His cap dislodged as he rolled and, laughing, he stretched out to grab it. Darren was laughing too and Jess soon joined in. The mood was lightening and I felt encouraged, though still not overly impressed with the level of the conversation.

'So which bit did you like best? Apart from the bit about the money and the presents.'

It was Darren who answered. 'Paul's family at the dinner table on Friday night was kinda neat,' he said. 'It was pretty emotional and made me feel good about being Jewish,' he added. I tried not to roll my eyes. It wasn't possible to have a conversation with anyone in this place without someone saying how something or other made them feel.

'One of my school friends who's not Jewish told me she was real jealous of me having a *bat-mitzvah*,' said Jess, absent-mindedly rolling a stalk of grass between the finger and thumb of her perfectly manicured right hand. The pink nail varnish was sprinkled with glitter.

'You can't actually have a *bat-mitzvah* – or a *bar-mitzvah* for that matter,' I said – and immediately regretted sounding so pompous and teacher-like.

'What?' exclaimed Josh, sitting himself up and rearranging his baseball cap to its preferred angle, precisely 180 degrees opposite where it was designed to be. His face was screwed up, showing disbelief that almost seemed to be anger, as if I was trying to mislead him – or someone already had.

'You become *bat* or *bar-mitzvah*,' I said, beginning to wish I hadn't started this. It was like pressing the play button on some old recording lodged inside my memory. 'According to the Rabbis of two thousand years ago, a boy is responsible for his own religious observances when he reaches the age of thirteen. Up till then, he's just practising. And a girl reaches that point at the age of twelve, because the Rabbis thought girls matured earlier –' Jess poked her tongue out at Josh who raised his hand in front of his face, middle finger aloft. I gave him one of my teacher's looks over the rim of my glasses and he held up his hands in mock innocence, as though the gesture had been a reflex.

I continued my well-rehearsed speech. 'Girls didn't have as many religious obligations as boys in the eyes of the Rabbis. They had too many other important things to do – like running the home and having children …' I waited for protests or laughs but none came. Were they listening or had I already lost them?

'But boys – well, men – had all sorts of *mitzvot* – commandments – to carry out that women were excused from. That's how they organised their society – women did the household stuff, men studied and prayed, and maybe did some work every now and then.' Jess looked hurt.

'It's no good looking at it from our twenty-first century perspective, Jess,' I said, holding out an appeasing hand. 'They saw things differently, that's all. And the boys learned Hebrew from a really early age, so they could be leading the service or reading from the Torah from about the age of six –'

'Six!' exclaimed Darren, genuine astonishment on his face. He shook his head vigorously, sending his dark hair to and fro. 'So why do we make such a big deal about doing this –' he picked up a see-through plastic folder containing a CD and some pages of Hebrew '- when we turn thirteen?'

I loved this bit. 'There's not really any need.' All three of them looked at me through suspicious, narrowed eyes. Josh's head was tilted slightly to one side and he was leaning forward, poised, as though preparing to attack me.

'A boy could do just about anything in the service as soon as he was able to,' I continued. 'But you may have heard of something called a *minyan*?' I looked at each of them, sensing a mixture of curiosity and hostility.

'Sure, the ten men thing that Orthodox Jews need to say certain prayers.' Darren's reply was impatient, almost contemptuous.

'Right – and you had to be over thirteen to count as a man, remember?' Vague nods. 'And you couldn't do a *mitzvah* till you were thirteen. And being called up to the Torah, saying the blessings, was a *mitzvah*, even though actually reading the Torah wasn't …' I paused and looked around them, enjoying my moment of triumph – though I wasn't really sure why I regarded it as such. 'Traditional Jewish services couldn't get past a certain point unless and until ten men were there,' I continued. 'So on the Saturday after a boy turned thirteen, he was called up to say the blessings during the Torah reading, which was a way of pointing a big finger at him and saying, "Next time you need a *minyan*, count this guy in from now on!"'

'That's it?' asked Darren, in a voice of squeaky disbelief.

'That's it,' I confirmed. Suddenly Josh jumped to his feet.

'Son of a bitch!' he yelled, throwing his folder to the ground in disgust and thrusting his hands into the pockets of his knee-length shorts. 'So why are they making us do this frigging stuff?'

Without looking back, he stomped off down the hill in the direction of the boys' cabins. Jess stretched her mouth tight across clenched teeth and raised her eyebrows apologetically at me; Darren stared at the ground.

'Oh dear,' I said, hoping that a bit of English understatement would cover my own shock and embarrassment at this unexpected outcome. 'I guess that's lesson over,' I added, after a short pause that seemed to go on for a very long time.

I watched as Jess and Darren awkwardly picked themselves up off the grass and gathered their folders. Darren gestured wordlessly with his stained white trainer at Josh's folder lying on the ground next to his foot.

'I'll hang onto it,' I said, and, trying to sound confident, added 'I'm sure he'll be back.'

I watched Jess and Darren head off in opposite directions towards their respective sections of the camp. 'Well, that could have gone better,' I muttered to no one in particular, lifting my eyes to the tree as I snapped the laptop shut. In the breezeless Saturday afternoon, I could have sworn the branches rustled as I walked away.

* * * * * * * * * * * *

11

The second encounter - Saturday night

In our next conversation, which took place later that evening, Isaiah agreed with me that it could indeed have gone better. It wasn't the first thing we discussed at what turned out to be a daily occurrence, as we reviewed and considered the significance of the ceremony for which I was supposedly preparing my young charges beneath the shade of the tree that spoke to me from the eighth century BCE.

We communicated with each other late at night, after the campers had all gone to their cabins. On that Saturday, following the extraordinary morning encounter and the lunchtime lesson, I had walked past the tree several times during the afternoon. I had cast furtive glances at it – through two eyes now, as my Isaiah costume had been abandoned – but there was no way I was going to resume a conversation with a tree while anyone else was looking. I wasn't even sure that I wanted to revisit the scene of my mysterious earlier encounter, but I found the whole episode intriguing, and was repeatedly drawn there, looking for some tell-tale sign of a biblical prophet concealed in its branches.

After the camp had said farewell to Shabbat with the ceremony of *havdalah*, I finally had the opportunity to continue our conversation of some twelve hours earlier. As I approached it – or should I say him? – I somehow knew that only now, only when the rest of the camp was at peace, would we be able to communicate. It had to be that way really. This was my secret – and if anyone actually saw me engaged in earnest discussion with a tree – well, even Californians may have baulked at that one. Maybe hugging a tree would be okay. But talking to one? No one ever saw us, which leaves me wondering to this day whether the whole thing was just a fantasy.

His opening shot when I approached that Saturday night was real enough. 'Perhaps you would be so kind as to explain what you were doing – and what you were wearing – this morning when last we spoke?' came the sarcastic voice. I gave a sort of nonchalant shrug as I explained about how I was being him, proclaiming the words of his vision in the opening chapter of the book that bore his name.

'And the thing on your face?' he insisted.

'Well,' I began hesitantly, 'the name *Yeshayahu* translates into English as Isaiah. And I'm pretending to be the prophet Isaiah – and so we have this little joke –' for God's sake, this joke was pathetic enough in front of any audience, but to a tree claiming to be or to contain Isaiah ...! '– that you have this name because one eye's 'igher than the other.'

'I suppose you find it amusing to go round pretending that I am a lunatic with a disfigured face? Isaiah indeed!' he snorted, emphasising the peculiarly English pronunciation of his name. I saw something move in the tree, and the moonlight shimmered through its branches, producing a strange, almost ethereal haze. Was he actually hiding in the branches of the tree? Or was he, in some unfathomable way, concealed within it? 'Besides, my name is *Yeshayahu* anyway,' he continued angrily, 'so that "eye's higher" wordplay does not work. A bit more substance and a bit less melodrama would not go amiss,' he said sternly.

It was my turn to hit back. 'Oh right,' I said, looking up at him but seeing only branches. 'This from the man who calls one of his sons "A Remnant Shall Return" and the other "Pillage Hastens, Looting Speeds" to make a point about the effects of Assyrian attacks.[2] You weren't averse to melodramatic public displays designed to cause an impact on your

---

[2] *she'ar yashuv*: Isaiah 7:3, *maher shalal hash baz* 8:3.

audience, were you? And at least I only used a sheet and a piece of card – you used your own children!'

There was a pause in which he seemed to be sizing me up, perhaps preparing to hurl his famous prophetic wrath at me. Then the branches rustled, carrying with them the unmistakable sound of laughter – and I laughed with him. The tension defused and I sat myself down, leaning against the bark of the tree.

'Anyway, never mind that,' he said, moving me away from any questions about how his sons might have felt, having been landed with such ridiculous names. 'I need to know more about this ceremony of *bar-mitzvah* that you talked about to your pupils this afternoon. What is this ceremony of which you spoke? It seemed to hold enormous power for the grandfather in the programme that you showed – though Josh appeared to have some difficulties with your explanation.'

A masterful understatement, I thought. 'Well, basically, they're going to be turning thirteen in a few months' time,' I explained, as though to a twelve-year-old. 'And Jewish tradition regards that age as having special significance, and as part of a ceremony to mark the occasion, encourages those reaching that age to read a section from the Torah and a *haftarah* in synagogue...'

'What is a *haftarah*?' he snapped, his tone suggesting resentment at having to have so much explained to him. So I explained how after the weekly reading from the Torah – an excerpt in Liberal synagogues, the whole section in Orthodox ones – an additional biblical reading, with a link to the Torah portion, was included. 'And that's always something written by you – the prophets,' I explained. 'A reading from the Torah and a reading from the prophets. That's what happens in synagogue every Shabbat and that's what I'm preparing those kids for.' As had happened earlier that morning, I had the impression that he was not understanding a word that I was saying.

'That is not what you said earlier,' he challenged. 'You said that any child could do that reading at any age.'

'Well, yes ...' I began.

'And the angry one did not like that, I seem to recall,' he continued. 'As you said to me at the time, that could have gone better.'

He was mocking me, I was sure of it. Or maybe Josh was hiding in the tree, getting his own back on me. Either way, I'd had enough. 'What is this?' I hissed, looking up at the unmoving branches. I wanted to shout but there were still one or two people around in camp and I didn't want to draw attention to myself. 'You're just winding me up. Don't try and kid me that I'm having some kind of mystical encounter with the biblical Prophet Isaiah or *Yeshayahu* or however you want to be referred to.' I strode angrily away from the tree but turned back after just three steps. 'And how come you speak English anyway?' I added. I was pointing accusingly at the tree, silhouetted against the clear, dark sky.

'I have no idea,' the voice sighed. 'Perhaps this connection across the ages is being made so that my message, the message that underpins the project I and my followers called the Torah of *YHWH* can be heard in your world. We recognised that there is a purpose to human life and we sought to understand what that purpose might be. And becoming an adult is a time to show a commitment to that quest, that search for meaning and purpose. What you call the Torah is a record of that exploration: it asks the questions and provides answers. Those are answers that were right two thousand and more years ago but in your age you have new answers, different understanding and knowledge.'

'Don't be too sure of that,' I said. 'There are many in my world who look at the text of the Torah and declare that it must all be true because it is written by God. Like the story of the world being made in six days ...'

'How can this be?' he said incredulously. 'How can anyone imagine that such stories were meant to be literal truth? That was an account of the creation of the world told by a wonderful storyteller from Shiloh in the northern kingdom of Israel. Jerusalem was full of such people in my lifetime because that kingdom was destroyed, wiped out by the Assyrians. They arrived with their stories and their visions, their history, their laws and their God. It was listening to them that made me realise how important it was that all this material should be recorded. The kingdom of Israel was no more but its search for meaning and for justice and for God should be preserved. This is how my work, the teaching project, began.'

'So you're saying that not even the author of the six-day creation story believed that he was writing about the true origins of the universe?' I enquired.

'Of course not,' replied the voice. 'He – or she – was just trying to get the audience to think about the origins of the planet and the place of God in their world.'

'So why does the story tell us the world was made in six days?' I asked.

'Because the Sabbath was observed every seventh day,' he replied. 'The story reflects the society that produced it, offering explanations for things that already existed, placing them in a context that the listeners could understand. How could anyone believe it was pretending to be literal truth?'

'So your work of teaching these children must begin,' he said, sounding earnest. 'How can this teaching, this Torah, continue to have meaning for those who listen to it if it is presented as being absolute truth? Challenge and question it so that you can discover that it is a quest for meaning and truth, not a manifestation of it.'

'The storytellers and the lawmakers of the north got some things wrong. We also got things wrong – of course we did. We knew so little. But we understood that there was a purpose to existence, and we tried to explain that to those who would listen to us. You know so much more than we did about the world. But your search for explanations has blinded you to the quest for meaning. That is what Torah represents and is: a quest for meaning.'

'How am I supposed to teach that?' I asked.

'You know what you must do,' he said slowly. 'You know that these children deserve to be introduced to a proper understanding of Torah – a genuine encounter rather than what was offered to you when you were their age. Be brave enough to challenge it, to take it apart and search for the truth of the questing human spirit that lies at its heart.'

'Where shall I start with such a project?' I asked.

'At the beginning,' he said simply. 'You know so much more about the origins of the universe than did we,' he continued. 'Start from what you know and believe about the world, just as we did. But remember that you are not only looking for explanation. You are also searching for meaning. And if you weren't able to do that,' he said with an air of finality, 'you wouldn't be sitting here having these thoughts and this conversation.'

I couldn't say for how long I sat there contemplating his words and the star-filled sky above me before I finally forced myself to rise and return to my cabin.

* * * * * * * * * * * * *

Back in my cabin, I made myself a coffee and sat down in front of my laptop and began to type out a lesson plan for the following day. The reflections on the origin of the biblical account of creation were still fresh in my mind. The purpose of this lesson was to get the students to think about the ways in which human beings ask questions about the origins of the universe and to recognise that the questions they ask and the answers they find are rooted in the society in which they live at a given point in history. A look at the creation stories in the bible gave an opportunity for discussion about the different literary sources of the biblical text. But it was also important to have a modern perspective on questioning the origins of the universe – what I needed was a way to introduce my students to our modern awareness of the vastness of the universe without blinding them with science. I flicked through the library of songs in my laptop's memory and found just what I was looking for…

* * * * * * * * * * *

LESSON TWO – Sunday afternoon

'In the Beginning ...'

It was hard to know where to start with this project. How exactly was I supposed to carry out the task that Isaiah had set me – leading these twelve-year-olds away from the inevitable rote learning of a few words in a foreign language with weird shaped letters that went *backwards*, for God's sake. And this ceremony just served as a prelude to overindulgence and the giving and receiving of material possessions that completely contradicted its very intention!

So I took the advice from the previous night and decided that, like all good projects – including the one around which this whole effort was based, this Torah – the place to begin was at the beginning. I went to our meeting place carrying four copies of the JPS *Tanakh*,[3] the Hebrew bible, some sheets of paper and a portable CD player. I lowered myself awkwardly to the ground to join the three students who were waiting there for me, seated beneath the tree with which I had shared such an extraordinary conversation the night before. They were not the same three who had been there twenty-four hours earlier. Darren and Jess were both there, dutifully clutching their plastic see-through folders with CDs and Hebrew texts. The third person turned out, after some questioning by me, to be Alison. Most of Alison's answers to my questions were contained in a single word, so it took some time to ascertain that she had apparently gone to the wrong place the day before and had been told by the rabbi that she wasn't on her list. With her chubby face, her protruding lower jaw that concealed a mouth brimming with metal, and thick glasses whose weight drove them down her nose requiring her constantly to push them up again, Alison gave the impression of not being on the list of any number of people. There was a sadness that emanated from her, a loneliness that emerged from behind an invisible protective wall that defied anyone to approach her.

I had no idea that the rabbis on the camp had even been given a list of their *bar-* and *bat-mitzvah* students. No one had given me such a list.

'Well, you can certainly be on my list, Alison,' I said, trying to sound as welcoming as possible. I could sense the resentment of Darren and Jess, though whether it was the intrusion or the nature of the intruder I could not tell. 'And where's Josh?' I ventured, looking at the two who had witnessed his angry departure the previous day. I had brought his *bar-mitzvah* folder with me – and it looked as though it would also return with me once this lesson was done, as both Darren and Jess shook their heads and shrugged.

I leaned back against the tree. 'Whatever,' I said, making a mental note to look for the absent Josh at some point later that Sunday.

---

[3] During the 'lessons' the students use the 1999 JPS (Jewish Publication Society) Bible (*Tanakh*). The extracts incorporated in the lesson plans at the end of the book are the author's own translations.

'We have much to get on with,' I said to my three students. 'Make yourselves comfortable – we're going on a fascinating journey to discover Torah!' I tried to sound like an enthusiastic tour guide.

'Aren't we just supposed to learn to read from it?' said Jess in a plaintive voice. 'We don't need to discover it – we know where it is.' She gestured at the auditorium a short distance up the hill, where yesterday's service had taken place. Darren laughed. Alison just stared at the ground.

'Ah, but do you know what it is?' I responded. And before any of them could say something dull about it being a long piece of parchment on two wooden rollers, containing Hebrew writing with no vowels, I added 'or why it is or ever came to be? Or who wrote it?'

'God wrote it,' said Alison, without looking up from the ground. Jess nodded her agreement. Darren looked slightly puzzled.

'Do you really think God writes books?' I said, and before any of them had a chance to respond, I handed each of them a copy of the Hebrew bibles I had brought with me. 'Let's see if we can work out how much of this God actually wrote,' I said. 'And let's start at the beginning ...'

Darren and Jess took it in turns to read the six days of creation from the first chapter of the book of Genesis. Darren got the odd numbered days, Jess the even ones – Alison had just shaken her head when it came to her turn.

'So what do you make of that?' I asked when the end of the sixth day had been reached and man and woman had been created. 'Does this sound to you like a true account of how the world started? And remember,' I added, 'according to Orthodox Jewish tradition, this all started on *Rosh ha-Shanah* less than six thousand years ago.'

'Well that can't be true,' objected Darren. 'I mean, we know that the world is more than six thousand years old. Way more. I mean – what about dinosaurs and stuff?' I nodded, hoping he would continue, but he was silent – though he was clearly still thinking. So was Jess, I could tell, but I couldn't see past Alison's invisible wall.

'You know that when the film – sorry, movie – 'Jurassic Park' came out, everyone went crazy about dinosaurs,' I said. 'They were everywhere – on t-shirts, bedding, lunchboxes. A dairy company in Israel brought out some yoghurts that featured dinosaurs – and their products were banned in ultra-Orthodox Jewish communities in Israel!'

'No way!' exclaimed Darren, a big grin broadening his thin face.

'Yes way!' I responded.

Jess looked puzzled. 'So how do they explain the existence of dinosaurs – or their bones?' she asked in a suspicious tone.

'I think they just say that God put them there to confuse us,' I replied. She rolled her eyes. 'But we know the Genesis story isn't true, not scientifically true,' I continued, sensing that

I had the interest and attention of at least two of my students. 'And we know much more about the place of our world in the grand scheme of things than whoever wrote the first chapter of Genesis three thousand years ago,' I added quickly. 'Yes, it was written by a person – I told you, God doesn't write books. And here's something written by another person, a song that I'd like you to listen to and think about.' I handed out a sheet to each of them containing the lyrics to Monty Python's 'Galaxy Song.' Alison's sheet remained on the floor in front of her where I placed it, but I saw her glance at it.

'Cool!' said Darren. 'We get to do Monty Python in our *bar-mitzvah* lesson!'

I clicked on the laptop and let Eric Idle sing to them about the unimaginable vastness of the universe and the tiny insignificant speck that we called planet Earth, our home.

The song ended and I quickly gave out another sheet of paper, one that contained a brief explanation of the scientific Big Bang theory of creation.

'So we know that God didn't just make the sun, moon and stars halfway through the creation process and place them in the sky as the first chapter of Genesis tells us,' I said as the participants looked at their sheets. Alison's was still by her side, but I was pretty sure she was looking. 'And thanks to our ability to look into the furthest corners of the universe, our science tells us that the world began with a massive explosion of energy rather more than six thousand years ago. Which of the two versions of creation do you think is more likely to be true? The bible's account?' Jess and Darren shook their heads vigorously; Alison's reaction was less noticeable but matched theirs. 'Or the scientific one?' All three nodded.

'Now I don't pretend to understand this stuff at all,' I said with a smile, waving the sheet of paper in the air with a shrug. 'But let me ask you a question with which you might be familiar. How does this scientific reality make you feel? What's it like to know that we live on a small, insignificant planet?'

'Kinda lonely,' said Jess, and for a moment I pictured her as a Country and Western singer, wearing a large cowboy hat and drawling the lyrics to a song about being 'kinda lonely'. Darren nodded his agreement, and to the astonishment of us all, Alison muttered, 'It makes me feel like no one cares about me.'

Ignoring the urge to give Alison a hug, I carried on. 'And what three things does the first chapter of Genesis give us that the scientific version can't?' All of them were clearly thinking hard.

'That there's a God?' Alison asked, tentatively.

'Exactly – that someone created the world,' I said and then, after a silence, 'and it tells us that this creator liked what had been made – each day ends with the words "*va-yar Elohim ki tov* – and God saw that it was good." And it also tells us that human beings were made in the image of that creator and placed at the pinnacle of creation – the very last things to be made.' I looked around and three faces were looking back at me, attentive now. 'Now that makes us feel a lot better about ourselves and the point of our lives than the Big Bang theory or the things we can see with the Hubble telescope.'

'So does that mean the first bit of the Torah isn't true?' asked Darren.

I smiled. ' Not the way we understand truth, no,' I said. 'But the person who wrote it – and we've already agreed that wasn't God because God doesn't write books, remember? The person who wrote it wasn't trying to write scientific truth. He – or she for that matter was doing exactly the same as the scientists who look through the Hubble telescope into the furthest corners of the universe are trying to do. Any guesses as to what that was?'

The three faces looked blank. I looked at each of them in turn but no answer emerged. It didn't matter. 'They were trying to answer questions that have been asked by every generation of human beings since we were able to ask questions. Why are we here? Who made this planet and put us here? What is the meaning of life?' I said, deliberately quoting the title of the film from which the song came. No one picked up the reference.

I lowered my arms and leaned forward. They seemed to lean forward too. 'And which of those accounts gives us a sense of purpose and meaning in our lives?' I asked, almost in a whisper. 'Stops us feeling kinda lonely,' I added.

'The Genesis story,' whispered Jess, a smile of understanding spreading across her face.

'Exactly!' I said. 'It's not meant to be true, it's meant to help us understand and appreciate something about ourselves and the purpose of our lives. And science can't do that, it's not interested in stuff like that. But the Big Bang theory and the first chapter of Genesis are both answers to ultimate questions about the origins of life, written three thousand years apart from totally different perspectives. They're both part of the human search for understanding about ourselves.'

I watched as two girls passed close by us, heading in the direction of their cabins, carrying their see-through plastic folders. The lunchtime study period was drawing to a close. I checked my watch – there were just ten minutes left of 'official' time. I needed to finish quickly – though I was pleased to note that there were no protests from my three students about the fact that others had already been released.

'Okay – turn back to your bibles and look at the second chapter of Genesis. Tell me what you make of this.' As time was short, I read the nine verses from the second chapter of Genesis. They began by telling how God had made man – Adam – from the dust before anything else. Only then did God plant trees and make all the other creatures, bringing them before Adam so he could name them all. God's intention was to find a companion for Adam but none of these creatures fitted the bill. So, in the well-known story, God put Adam into a deep sleep, took one of his ribs and made woman – Eve.

'What do you make of that?' I asked. We had to go quickly now – people were beginning to emerge from their cabins. The after lunch break was over and the first session of the afternoon was about to begin. Jess was looking up the hill at groups of girls, looking for friends.

'Just two minutes,' I pleaded.

'But all this has already been created!' exclaimed Darren. 'Why is God doing it again?'

'Exactly!' I replied, speaking quickly, urgently. 'I'll tell you, 'cause we're out of time. This was a different account of how the world began – another answer to the same question about where we came from, answered by someone else. We know it was written by a different person, and not just because it tells a different story about creation. Look back at the first chapter. Who was doing all the creating?' They all flicked back a page.

It was Alison who answered first, seeming to grasp what I was getting at. 'God,' she said.

'Right,' I agreed. 'Now look at the bit I just read you. Who was in charge of that?' They flicked the page again.

'The LORD God!⁴' Alison again, which I was pleased to note.

'Or the Eternal God, as we now prefer to say. Two different stories about the creation of the world written by two different people who call God by a different name,' I explained.

'So you're telling us the Torah was written by lots of people?' said Alison. I nodded. 'If that's true, why do we treat it so specially?' Darren was nodding. 'And read from it with all that ceremony and stuff?' she went on, before sinking into silence.

'It's just a book, written by people,' added Jess.

'Of course it's written by people,' I said. 'As I said before, God doesn't write books. God gives us the ability to think, inspires us to ask questions about our world and ourselves, encourages us to look for meaning in our lives. But the answers we come up with are all ours, based on how we experience the world. The person who wrote what came to be the first chapter of Genesis probably lived in a society where every seventh day was a day of rest. And that person also lived in a society that referred to God as *Elohim*. So that author's answer to how the world was created was built upon how he or she and those around them saw and understood the world. The author of the second chapter of Genesis lived in a society where God was referred to as *YHWH Elohim* and was trying to explain something else about the creation of the world.' There was no time to refer back to the text and ask any more questions so I had to complete this part of the lesson myself.

'After the woman has been made from the man's rib, the chapter ends with the words "Therefore a man will leave his father and mother and be joined with his wife, and they will become one flesh".⁵ So what is the author of this version of the creation story trying to explain?'

'Why women are dependant on men?' ventured Darren.

'Yeah, right!' snapped Jess. 'In your dreams!'

---

⁴ The translation in the 1999 JPS *Tanakh* translates *YHWH* as LORD; modern Liberal practice translates this as 'Eternal' or 'the Eternal One' (see translations on p.130).
⁵ Genesis 2:24

'And in ancient societies, I'm afraid Jess,' I said. 'There isn't time to go into it right now but the truth is that for most of human history and with very few exceptions, women have been less powerful than men.

'So what we have here are not accounts that were meant to be true – not as we understand truth in our time,' I continued. 'They're myths. Stories that are constructed to make people think about their lives and to give them a sense of purpose and an awareness of something greater than themselves that can give depth and significance to their lives.' I looked at my little group, whose expressions were thoughtful.

'Now go, or you'll be late for the first afternoon session!'

The three students stood up, picking up their folders. 'Do we need to bring these tomorrow?' asked Jess, as though carrying a lightweight folder was the most dreadful imposition. I shook my head, smiling.

'Just a questioning mind,' I replied. They all turned and walked away, smiling.

'Well, that went better.' I winked at the tree as I gathered up the bibles and the laptop.

The third encounter – Sunday night

'Well, that went better.' I suppose I shouldn't really have been surprised that our conversation seemed to pick up exactly where it had left off, no matter how much time passed between my visits to this tree. Maybe time paused while I wasn't there – who knows. It didn't really matter anyway – the whole thing was beyond understanding.

He spoke to me at the very moment I arrived there. It was later – almost midnight. A quarter moon hung in a clear sky, surrounded by more stars than I normally saw from my home in England. Less artificial light blocking them out, up here in the hills of northern California, though there were still fewer to be seen from here than from the wilderness of ancient Judah, where human technology had not yet impacted on the beauty of the universe.

'So tell me more about this Big Bang theory,' he said as I seated myself, adjusting my position.

'I don't know!' I exclaimed. 'I'm a rabbi, not a scientist. You heard the song, which makes clear just how small and insignificant this planet of ours is?' He murmured his agreement. 'Then you know about as much as I do,' I said, feeling that maybe I'd let the twenty-first century down by not being able to explain the Big Bang theory.

'It does not matter. Tell me, what were you saying about dinosaurs and yoghurt?'

I laughed – the idea of a Tyrannosaurus Rex sitting down to a pot of yoghurt amused me. How would it get the lid off? I began to explain how dinosaurs had roamed the earth millions of years ago, then interrupted myself.

'Hang on, I have a better idea. Here's a thing I would have done with the kids but there just wasn't time. And time is what this is all about.' I asked him to imagine that the entire history of the world from the Big Bang to that moment was condensed into just a year, where the Big Bang had occurred at midnight on January 1st and where we were at that moment was exactly a year later, at midnight on December 31st. I thought about doing it based on the Jewish calendar but I didn't think I'd be able to do the months properly. So I stuck to the Gregorian calendar, even though he probably wouldn't have a clue what I was talking about. The first fish appeared about a week before the end of November. The dinosaurs arrived on December 10th and were extinct by December 25th. The earliest human beings turned up on the afternoon of December 31st, and Isaiah himself arrived about twenty seconds ago. I'd been here for about 0.04 – four hundredths – of a second.

'Think of that,' I said. 'On the scale of the history of the earth as one year, you and I are separated by just a few seconds. This planet has a long history and we are such a tiny part of it, just like we're such a tiny part of the vast universe.'

'Which is why it is so important that we try to search for meaning in our lives,' he said. 'You did well, explaining the significance of the Genesis creation story, by the way,' he added. I had a vague sense that he was patronising me, though it was difficult to grasp his attitude when all I had was a voice reaching me through the branches of the tree above and behind me from a place maybe deep within it that was almost three thousand years away – however brief such a period of time might be in the larger scheme of things.

'So is that what Torah is?' I asked. 'A search for meaning?' I could think of several bits of the Torah that didn't seem to represent a search for anything and some that were searching for things that might have been better left alone.

'What about something like the story of Noah and the flood?' I suggested, working my way mentally through the early legends of the book of Genesis. 'I mean I can understand how the story of Adam, Eve and the serpent is about human sexuality and how Cain and Abel symbolise human rivalry – but where does Noah fit into the scheme of things? God decides to wipe everything out and start all over again? But God chooses one man and his family to survive and gets him to collect pairs of animals and put them in a large boat – it's not easy to find meaning in that, is it?'

'All those ancient stories are the reworking of ancient legends that were told and re-told throughout all the local kingdoms,' he said simply. 'Each storyteller made his or her particular god the deity who controlled the human beings who were part of the story. And the story – especially one like Noah and the flood – was one that was based on something that had actually happened. How else would every kingdom and empire in the area have its own version of a flood that wiped out everyone except for one person and enough animals to start it all over again?'

I listened in silence.

'The story of Noah – which also came from Shiloh – is based upon a dreadful flood that wiped out a civilisation. It happened hundreds of years before my time. The story was used to point out that human wickedness gets punished by the Eternal One. We had a version of it, the Assyrians had a version of it – everyone did. It was a useful thing to frighten people with, that's all. I'm sure that if you do some research you'll find all the evidence you need to prove that there was a flood that is the basis of all these stories.

'Telling stories was really important. It was the only form of entertainment the people had,' he continued. 'And the stories that were told had a basis in reality, they were built around the people's experiences. That's why it made sense to encapsulate the work of creation into six days – the people were already familiar with the idea of working for a six-day period and resting on the seventh day. And everyone knew that there had once been a flood, so it was a useful basis for a story.'

'And everyone knew what a rainbow was as well,' I added, 'so the storyteller just wove that in as part of the story.'

'Precisely,' he agreed. 'Though no one knew how rainbows were formed, so it just added weight to the idea that God was behind the whole flood incident.'

I briefly explained, to the best of my very limited scientific knowledge, how rainbows were formed by the rays of the sun refracting the drops of rain but he didn't seem to understand – probably because I wasn't very clear what I was talking about.

'I prefer the biblical storyteller's explanation,' he said. 'As with the creation story, it may not be what you would call scientific truth, but it encourages us to think about God and our world and gives us a sense of meaning and purpose.'

'There are plenty who believe that it is scientific truth,' I said. 'Would you believe that we even have people who claim to have found remnants of Noah's ark somewhere in the modern country of Turkey?'

'This is alarming,' came the voice from somewhere behind me. 'Listening to your scientific explanations of the origins of the world, I thought that the human race had moved on. Now it sounds as though you have gone backwards – turning the stories we developed to teach people about what God wanted of them into stories that God actually wrote about real things that happened? How can humanity have done that?'

'You think that's bad,' I laughed. 'You should hear what they've done with some of your material.'

'What?' he demanded.

'Well, you know the bit where you anticipated the birth of Hezekiah – "the young woman will conceive" and all that?' [6]

'He was a good king,' said the prophet, 'one of the few in my lifetime who was.' He treated me to a short history lesson, explaining his role in the palace of the kings of Judah during a time of political upheaval in the area we now call the Middle East. Isaiah was often called upon to advise the king of Judah and help them formulate their foreign policy with regard to the large empires of Egypt and, in particular, Assyria to the north as well as dealing with their local, and often troublesome, neighbours, Israel and Syria.

'Well, those words got taken to be a prediction that hundreds of years after you, a virgin would miraculously conceive a son who was directly descended from God – the one you called "Wonderful Counsellor, Mighty God, Everlasting Father and Prince of Peace."' [7]

'They said it meant WHAT?' he roared. The tree was shaking and I moved away from it – startled by the suddenness of the motion. 'All I was doing was heralding the birth of Hezekiah and predicting that the threatened invasion of Syria and Israel would be over by the time his pregnant mother had given birth – which is exactly what happened.' The branches of the tree shook. I imagined the prophet shaking his head in disbelief. 'And these would be the same people who believe that the world was made in six days, I suppose,' he continued, heavy sarcasm in his voice.

'It gets worse,' I whispered. 'Just see what's coming up later this week. Remember I told you about *Tish'ah b'Av*? Well, it's about more than just Solomon's Temple being destroyed. You'll find out things about the human race that will make you ashamed to be a part of it.' I shook my head slowly, anticipating the ancient prophet's reaction to Wednesday night's service which would recall the memories of so many centuries of the brutal treatment of his descendants by others. The fact that the origins of that brutality lay in the misinterpretation of scriptures, many of which were authored by Isaiah, was an irony that I found difficult to grasp.

'But meanwhile, let me put the story of Noah right,' I said, trying to sound more cheerful. I pushed myself up from the ground, instinctively turning to face the tree, even though I couldn't see him in it. It was getting late, I needed to get some sleep and I didn't want to walk away on such a negative note. 'Tomorrow I'll check out the internet and see if I can find out proof that will enable me to explain what really happened and to point out to these kids how important it is to look for the messages about human behaviour and responsibility that lie behind these stories.'

* * * * * * * * * * * *

---

[6] Isaiah 7:14

[7] Isaiah 9:6

I didn't want to wait until tomorrow. Instead of returning to my cabin, I headed for the education building – which was really a wooden hut – which housed a number of computers linked to the internet. Sure enough, I found that there was a Babylonian story called the Epic of Gilgamesh which dated from the third millennium BCE and which told the story of a devastating flood. Then I looked for details of a devastating flood about five thousand years ago – and found that recent archaeological evidence had been discovered that showed that the Black Sea had once been a low-lying lake with a sophisticated civilisation on its shore that was suddenly devastated when the Mediterranean Sea flooded into it about six or seven thousand years ago.

I was struggling to stay awake, so I printed off information from these various websites and stumbled back to my cabin, thinking about how to present this wealth of material. I hoped to find ways to make my students think of how such stories endured as they were passed from generation to generation; how they varied from one culture to another and no matter how improbable a tale might seem, there might well be a grain of truth at its core. The secret, I thought to myself, was to scrape away all the elements that had been added to a story to embellish it and find the facts on which it was based in order to be able to discover the lesson it was seeking to teach.

LESSON THREE – Monday afternoon

'The animals went in seven by two …'

I was looking forward to this lesson, so I got there early. I had five copies of the *Tanakh* with me - rather optimistically I hoped that Josh would return. I had checked with the camp administration and had been told that Josh's parents were quite insistent that a rabbi should work with him on his preparation for his *bar-mitzvah* ceremony while he was at camp – even though that ceremony wasn't due to take place until the following March. Poor kid. I was beginning to get a sense of where his anger was coming from … At the same time I had also found out that Alison wasn't meant to be in my group at all, but clearly the rabbi to whom she had been assigned figured that someone else could deal with this difficult girl.

I looked up and saw her shuffling down the path from the girls' cabins. She looked so sad, so alone.

I took the laptop out of its bag and opened it up. 'Here we go,' I said, glancing up at the branches of the tree under whose shade I had placed my resources but no answer came. It seemed that, apart from our first encounter, which had so surprised both of us, he only spoke under cover of darkness. But I sensed his presence and the memory of last night's conversation, along with my early morning internet research encouraged me as I prepared to dismantle another quaint little biblical story – Noah, the flood, and the animals going in two by two …

'Hey Rabbi!' It was Darren, who had arrived from the boys' cabins.

'Hey Darren,' I replied. 'Any news of Josh?'

He shook his head slowly. 'I haven't seen him since yesterday so I can't really say,' he said. I nodded and gestured for him to sit under the shade of the tree. Clearly I was going to have to take the matter of Josh and his participation in this group a little higher. Although she was the first I had seen approaching, Alison managed to arrive last, her slow shuffle preceded by Jess's high speed arrival.

'Let's get started guys,' I said as soon as they were seated. 'We have a lot to get through today and we almost ran out of time yesterday. Let's start by watching this – can you all see the screen okay?' I waited for the three of them to adjust their positions, then I pressed play. The title page showed them that they were about to watch 'Children's Bible Stories' and I quickly selected Noah and the Flood and pressed enter. I didn't see the need for any further introduction.

It was a predictable and deliberately chosen literal dramatisation of the story that occupied chapters 6 – 9 of the book of Genesis. Well literal, save for the fact that Noah and his family were white-skinned and spoke English with American accents – an astonishing linguistic achievement that even extended to some of the animals. It was interesting to note how engrossed the students were, proving that showing them moving pictures on a screen was the easiest way to keep their attention. I don't imagine they would have been so focused had I chosen simply to read them a children's version of the story.

'So you remember the story?' I asked. They all nodded.

'It's kinda cute,' said Jess, with a kinda cute smile.

'And do you remember the songs you learned about this story when you were little?' I continued. 'Who built the ark? Noah! Noah!' They were all joining in before I had even reached the end of the first line. I let it continue for a little longer but brought the singing to an end just as Jess looked as though she might get up and start marching around the tree. Even Alison had been singing and there was a hint of a smile on her face. Powerful stuff …

'This is some *bar-/bat-mitzvah* group!' I exclaimed, jokingly. 'Everyone else is reading Hebrew and learning their blessings and we're watching TV and singing kindergarten songs!' Suddenly my three twelve year–olds looked sheepish.

'Oh don't be so embarrassed,' I chided. 'Everyone likes to sing a silly song every now and then.'

'Yeah but it's not very grown up – and isn't that what *bar-* and *bat-mitzvah* is meant to be?' protested Darren.

'Okay,' I said. 'You want grown up? Listen to this.' A couple of clicks on the laptop and Bill Cosby's sketch of an imaginary conversation between God and Noah was playing.

'That was funny!' exclaimed Jess, when I stopped the CD.

'Yes. But why was it funny?' I asked.

'Well the situation was just dumb,' said Darren thoughtfully. 'I mean, a voice comes out of nowhere and tells a guy that the world is going to be destroyed and he should build a big boat and take two of every animal on it. Anyone would have to be crazy to listen to that. And the fact that Noah questions it is what makes it funny, 'cause by challenging it, he makes it sound, well, ridiculous,' he said, uncertainty in his voice.

'You're saying that a story in the Torah is ridiculous?' I boomed with mock anger. Darren looked alarmed.

'Well, no ...' he stammered.

'Well yes, actually,' I replied, smiling at him, quickly adding 'and that's fine. Look, yesterday we agreed that the story of creation as described in Genesis chapter one couldn't be true, and we saw that it's contradicted in chapter two anyway. And we worked out that those two versions of the creation story were written by two different people, with a different name for God who probably didn't know each other – who probably lived in different places,' I added, recalling Isaiah's words about Israelite storytellers.

'And let's be honest,' I continued, 'can the story of Noah really be true?'

'Well, there's only one version of it,' came an unexpected voice. It was Alison. She recoiled as if her own words had shocked her.

'Well yes and no, Alison,' I said hesitantly. 'In the Torah, yes, pretty much. But there are stories of gods sending floods in other cultures as well. Take a look at this – ' I handed out a sheet of paper containing details about the Epic of Gilgamesh. 'There was a story written around the same time as our Noah story. Its main theme was a flood being sent to punish people and one man being selected to survive by building a large boat. As you can see from the chart, there were quite a few differences between the two stories – not least the names of the heroes. Our man Noah becomes Utnapishtim in the Babylonian version.' That got a laugh. 'And because Babylonians worshipped lots of gods, their story has the flood happen because these gods were annoyed with human beings - and Utnapishtim even gets to become a god at the end. But our version reflects the fact that the Israelites were trying to encourage a belief in just one God – a God who wanted people to be good – like Noah.

'But the theme of a great flood – and someone surviving it and saving the animals – is in both stories,' I continued. 'So what does that make you think?'

'That there really was a great flood?' said Jess cautiously, as though it was a trick question and she was saying something foolish.

'Absolutely right,' I said and a broad smile filled Jess's face. Darren raised his eyebrows to indicate that he wasn't as impressed with Jess's powers of deduction as she was.

'At some point in history, a terrible flood must have occurred. It caused great destruction and left its mark on the memories of the people who lived nearby. It made such an impression that they made up stories about it, changing the names of the characters and some of the other details to fit their particular language, religion or culture. But the actual flood was in all the stories. Take a look at the map underneath the chart,' I said, indicating the map of the Mediterranean Sea and the lands on its eastern coast. 'See this narrow gap between the Mediterranean and the Black Sea?' I half stood, leaning across to each of them in turn to make sure they were looking at the right place.

'Okay. We know from archaeology that what is now the Black Sea used to be separated from the Mediterranean by a piece of land. Behind that piece of land, the Black Sea was a low level lake and there was a very well developed civilisation living on its shores. Then suddenly, one day – maybe as a result of some kind of global warming or just unusual weather conditions – the sea level rose and this land bridge just gave way. The Mediterranean

Sea poured in, instantly wiping out an entire civilisation. Bang!' I clapped my hands to denote the instantaneous effect of this catastrophe. Alison and Jess looked up in shock; Darren laughed.

'In the last ten years or so, archaeologists have studied the floor of the Black Sea and have found remnants of that civilisation. They estimate that it was wiped out around seven thousand years ago. And six or seven thousand years ago, word spread that this catastrophic flood had happened and it left its mark in the memories of the people living at that time. So much so that they told stories about it, seeing it as some kind of punishment because people had upset whatever gods they happened to believe in. Are you still with me?'

Actually I knew they were; I could see they were listening. All three nodded. 'Can you think of any recent natural catastrophes that people might interpret as being some kind of punishment from an angry god?'

'Oh my God – Hurricane Katrina!' exclaimed Jess, wide-mouthed.

'Exactly,' I replied. 'And even though we know exactly why it happened, thanks to our knowledge of meteorology, there are still people who are trying to tell us it was some kind of divine punishment. Like the Israeli Sephardi Chief Rabbi who said it happened to New Orleans because not enough black people studied Torah!'

We all laughed, then Darren said, 'And the Asian tsunami ...'

There was a sort of awed silence as we all thought back to that December morning when news of that devastating tidal wave had splashed across our world's media and we watched helplessly as hundreds of thousands perished while survivors saw their homes washed away.

'Nature can be very cruel,' I said 'and as we'll see later, it often helps people to understand it if they see God's hand at work in it. It may be that in Thailand or New Orleans, stories about those disasters will be told hundreds of years from now. At least they'll have TV images and photographs to show what happened. All they had four, five, six thousand years ago were the stories they told each other – and they varied depending on the storyteller – and the audience.'

I was on a roll now so I just kept going. Darren and Jess were looking at me; Alison had a thoughtful expression and seemed to be picking her nose.

'Remember, storytelling was a big deal back in those days. It was the only form of entertainment for a start, and in order to make it entertaining, the person telling the story would have to make it work for the audience. And some storytellers were trying to teach the people a lesson too. So whoever got hold of the story of

the flood in ancient Israel wanted to use it to tell people that God punished wickedness.'

The camp was showing signs of coming back to life for the afternoon. Time was running out again. I pressed on.

'And it was a great story. The Israelite version, with our man Noah and their God, *Elohim*, was first put together maybe three thousand years ago. And we still know it pretty much by heart. Not only that –' I gestured towards the laptop '– but three thousand years later a comedian can stand up on stage and do a sketch about it – tell a story if you like – and we all know exactly who and what he's talking about. See how powerful stories are?'

All three were looking at me now and they were nodding. It appeared that my storytelling was working too. 'That doesn't mean the story was true, it wasn't talking about things as they actually happened. It took something that people were familiar with and told it in a way that could teach them something about themselves and their world. And good stories survived, were told over and over again until they became part of a people's folklore. They became myths – stories that weren't true but which sort of explained to people who they were and where they belonged. This is big stuff,' I said, recognising that time was running out, 'and we'll be coming back to the question of why people need to have myths, why they need to have a sense of who they are and where they belong. But one more thing before we finish if that's okay with you.'

I reached for the bibles and handed one to each of them, noting the extra, unused copy for the still absent Josh. 'We watched a modern cartoon version of this, we sang a children's song about it and we heard a comedy sketch based on it. Let's just finish off with a look at the actual text of the story as it has been handed down for hundreds of years. Genesis, chapter 6, verse 9. Darren?'

Darren dutifully read the well-known verses about Noah being told to build the ark, its dimensions, the gathering of the animals two by two and the instruction to take food for the voyage. 'Thanks Darren,' I said. 'All pretty familiar stuff, right?' Three heads nodded. 'Okay. Would one of you ladies like to read the first three verses of chapter seven?' To my surprise – and delight – Alison began to read, jumping in ahead of Jess. I could hear the surprise in her voice, and I saw it in the listeners' faces, as she read the Lord[8]'s instructions to Noah to take seven pairs of every clean animal.

'Where did that come from?' exclaimed Darren.

'You see, that's not in the bit we learned,' I said. 'No one taught us that some of the animals went in seven by two …'

'What's that about?' protested Jess, sounding almost angry that someone had messed with the story. Someone <u>had</u> messed with the story, as I was about to tell them.

'Let's do what we did with those two creation stories yesterday. Look who's giving Noah the instructions in chapter six.'

---

[8] See note 4 p.20.

'God!' all three of them exclaimed, almost simultaneously, though I think Alison was first.

'That's *Elohim* again, the same God who made the world in chapter one. And who's talking in chapter seven?'

'The Lord!' said Alison. 'Exactly,' I said, enjoying the looks of understanding that spread across their faces. 'And the Lord is telling Noah to make sure he takes seven pairs of every clean animal and two of those that are unclean – a distinction that God in chapter six didn't bother to make.'

'What's that about?' protested Jess.

'Well that bit was added later by someone who wanted to make sure that the people didn't think that Noah was eating non-kosher food on board the ark. That someone lived and worked in a place where God's name was 'the Lord', while the original storyteller came from the same place – or was maybe even the same person – who told the six-day creation story. More proof that the Torah was written by different people, not by Moses or God.'

I closed the bible. 'That's it for today, folks,' I said, noting that all other *bar-/bat-mitzvah* lessons had long since disbanded.

They stood up, stretching as they did and dusting down their clothes.

'Why are you telling us all this?' asked Jess, a puzzled frown across her brow. 'I mean, everyone else is just reading bits of their portion during these lessons.'

'You can read your Torah portion anytime,' I replied, snapping the laptop shut. 'And when the time comes, you'll read it fine. But I want you to know what it is you're reading, where it came from and why. Cool?'

'Cool,' she replied and turned to run up the hill.

The fourth encounter – Monday night

I didn't really have anywhere else to take my anger so an invisible ancient Israelite prophet in a tree seemed as good a place as any. I'd been seething since late afternoon when I had been summoned by the head of faculty at camp – the rabbi in charge of the rabbis there. Not only that, she had arranged for Josh to be there too – he who had walked out of my lesson so dramatically two days earlier. Apparently Josh had complained that I wouldn't listen to him read his portion and that I'd told him that he didn't have to have a *bar-mitzvah* ceremony anyway.

The head of faculty, who was younger than me by several years but who had been coming to that camp every year since she was about seven years old had explained to me that if parents specifically requested that the rabbis on camp take time to help their children prepare their *bar-mitzvah* portions, then we had to honour that. And that meant hearing them read the Hebrew, not showing them DVDs of old sitcoms. I briefly tried to defend my approach to teaching *bar-* and *bat-mitzvah*, based on the content of my nocturnal encounters. It soon dawned on me, however, that any mention of the prophetic influence might not increase my chances of persuading her that my teaching methods had merit, so I quickly conceded defeat and listened silently. Throughout the whole conversation, Josh was glowering at me as though I was the enemy and he had scored some major victory over me. It was as though he felt that being made to read Hebrew every lunchtime was something worth fighting for ...

The prophet was silent while I vented my fury. I didn't know if he was listening.

'So what will you do with Josh when he comes back tomorrow?' he finally asked. 'Maybe I'll get him to read the Torah blessings before we discuss some more of those Genesis stories,' I said.

'What blessings are these?' he asked.

'The ones I told the kids about the other day – the ones before and after the Torah reading, which can only be read by someone once they turn thirteen.'

'Oh yes – the only part of a *bar-* or *bat-mitzvah* ceremony that has any significance – a fact that really upset Josh.' He laughed. 'What do these blessings say?'

I ran through the blessings in my mind and selected the key phrase, which occurred in the blessing that followed the reading of the Torah: *asher natan lanu torat emet* – words of praise to God 'who gave us teachings of truth'.

'Basically they thank God for giving us the Torah and how we recognise that everything in it is true,' was my summary. He laughed again.

'I think not,' he said. 'We have just spent the last two days talking about the world being made in six days and Noah building an ark to save all the animals and now you're telling me that before and after you read these stories, you have to declare thanks that it's all God's truth?' The branches of the tree were shaking. 'That's a bit ironic ...' I laughed with him.

'So tell me what these students of yours are going to be reading from this Torah, these true things that they are going to thank God for,' he continued, his voice laden with irony.

'Well, as I recall, Jess is celebrating her *bat-mitzvah* ceremony in September and she's doing something nightmarish from the end of Deuteronomy – the consequences of observing the terms of the covenant. She gets to do the short list of good things that will follow if the people observe the laws in that book – not the much longer list of bad things that will happen if they don't. And that's not pleasant reading....' I paused, but he said nothing so I carried on with my list. 'Darren's got Jacob's dream at Beth-El and Josh has got some weird Levitical rules about sacrifices. God help whoever has to explain that to him,' I snorted. 'Not sure about Alison as I don't even think she's meant to be in my group,' I concluded.

'So let me see if I'm getting this right,' he said. 'These young people are reading these sections from the Torah to demonstrate that they're now responsible adult members of the Jewish community and the key element of this is a blessing that thanks God for these true teachings that they are reading?'

'That's the idea, yes.' I was actually getting a bit irritated, which surprised me. I sensed that he was mocking our modern religious practices. 'Look it may be flawed, but it's an attempt to ensure that this religion has a future,' I said, surprised to find myself defending the ceremony of *bar-* and *bat-mitzvah*. Particularly in this country, where over-the-top celebrations were the norm. I had heard stories of a *bat-mitzvah* girl being brought on the back of a white horse into the room where the celebration dinner was taking place, and I had seen some pretty garish events back home as well. They seemed to miss the point completely – just an excuse for a party. Putting too much emphasis on the *bar* and not enough on the *mitzvah*, as the cliché went.

'In the Liberal movement in my country, we got rid of *bar-mitzvah* when we were first established just over a hundred years ago. In its place we introduced a confirmation ceremony called *Kabbalat Torah* – a group ceremony for our kids when they completed their Jewish education at about the age of sixteen. A much more reasonable time for kids to be acknowledging their commitment to this ancient faith,' I said, conscious that I was beginning to sound like some kind of advertisement.

'You keep referring to Orthodox and Liberal,' he said. 'You must explain to me the distinction to which you refer.' I nodded, relishing the opportunity. 'But right now,' he continued, 'we need to think about what to do about Josh.'

'Well strangely, his complaint seems to be that we're not practising any Hebrew reading,' I said, glad of the opportunity to discuss this situation with someone other than faculty members. 'But if I asked him to read Hebrew, he'd probably run a mile. I don't understand.'

'So why do you not ask him to read some Hebrew?' came the voice of wisdom from the tree. 'Perhaps those blessings about which he is so concerned? Then we might see what his real problem is.'

'I know what his real problem is,' I said. 'His parents are pushing him to do his *bar-mitzvah* ceremony, and he's terrified of what'll happen if he goes home and he can't read any more of it than he could when he got here. Which I wouldn't mind betting is nothing at all,' I added.

'We had a good solution for children like him in my day,' said the voice from the tree. 'If they were stubborn and rebellious like your Josh, we would threaten to take them to the elders of the city and have them stoned to death.'

'That was one of your ideas?' I asked in disbelief. 'It was a bit extreme, wasn't it?' How could the verses from the book of Deuteronomy about capital punishment for misbehaving children be part of Isaiah's teaching?

'Oh it was never carried out,' he laughed. 'But children could never be sure that it would not be.' His voice became more serious. 'After all, deliberately killing children was not unknown in my day.'

'That's why I'm going to get them to think about the story of Abraham sacrificing Isaac tomorrow – among other things,' I said. 'I assume that was written to demonstrate the folly of child sacrifice?'

'I do not know what you mean,' he replied. 'Who sacrificed whom?' I screwed up my face and mouthed 'What?' into the darkness. Even though I didn't say it aloud, he spoke as though he had heard me.

'Many of the stories that you have talked about in what you call the Torah,' he began, sounding like an impatient teacher explaining a simple concept to a confused child, 'were put together long after my death. Much of this material is new to me. It did not exist in the time and the place in which I lived and worked. Tell me something about these people you mentioned.'

Struggling to conceal my astonishment that I was having to tell him about the biblical patriarchs, I offered as brief a summary of some of the stories of Abraham and Sarah, Isaac and Rebekah, and Jacob, Leah and Rachel as I could manage. Included in my list was Abraham's departure from his home to travel to the land of Canaan, the story of Sodom and Gomorrah, the birth of Isaac and the childhood arguments of Jacob and Esau. I was about to launch into the story of Joseph and his brothers when he stopped me.

'It is as I would have expected,' he declared. 'The stories that talk of the exploits of these ancestors had a very specific purpose. They were designed to give those listening to them a sense of their origins and identity. It is interesting that you mentioned that the character called Abraham had a conversation with God about the destruction of Sodom and Gomorrah. Just like Noah: another example of a known historical event – two cities destroyed by an earthquake – being connected with an individual who features in the tradition of a particular people. And the promise of the land being given to these patriarchal figures would have been an essential part of reminding the listeners that they had a place where they belonged. Perhaps it was even a place to which they would one day return from a period of exile,' he added thoughtfully.

After a pause, he announced 'I should like to know more of these stories. We can work together to ascertain their import and their purpose.'

'Then you should also become part of my *bar-/bat-mitzvah* group, *Yeshayahu ben Amoz*,' I said with mock grandeur. 'You can sit next to Josh,' I added.

'It will be a pleasure,' he replied.

'Well,' I said, as I rose to my feet to go to my bed. 'Have I got some stories for you!'

* * * * * * * * * * * *

The walk back to my cabin was a pleasant one, filled with images of the various stories from Genesis that would form the basis of tomorrow's lesson. The thought of trying to re-integrate Josh into the group troubled me though. I decided to begin the lesson in a way that he might have expected – with basic practice of the Torah blessings, before presenting some of the stories and asking the students how they felt about declaring such stories to be God's truth.

By the time I stepped through the door, the shape of the lesson had already formed in my mind. It was a quick task to type it all out and then I headed for bed.

LESSON FOUR – Tuesday afternoon

'Tell us a story.'

Sure enough, there he was. Josh stood in the shade of the tree, dutifully clutching the folder that had made its way back to him after I had handed it in to the office three days earlier. That was the office in which our meeting had taken place, when I had been told that I had a responsibility to prepare these young people for their forthcoming *bar-* and *bat-mitzvah* ceremonies. And that was exactly what I was doing, I thought to myself as I approached the tree. And it would take more than Josh, his parents and head of faculty to talk me out of that. 'After all,' said the voice inside my head, 'I have Isaiah to back me up.'

'Hi, Josh!' I said cheerfully as I reached the tree. He looked anxious, much less confident than he had done the previous afternoon. His round face looked red, seeming to show some sign of embarrassment, as if he felt as though he'd got me into trouble and I was going to exact my revenge in some way. He was chewing hard. Poor kid. I decided to put him out of his misery. 'I think you're the first twelve-year-old who has ever asked for the opportunity to practise Hebrew during the *m'nuchah*' He laughed, a little too loudly I thought.

'Look, it's okay,' I said, trying to settle him down. He looked as though he was about to run away again. Fortunately Jess arrived, followed by Alison. The former greeted Josh with a predictably overbearing and surprisingly sincere sounding 'Hey Josh! Good to see you!' Alison said nothing, though to be fair, she probably didn't know who he was.

Darren arrived soon afterwards and nodded to Josh, who had already assumed his position of being almost flat out on his back. The two girls had also sat down, so Darren and I joined them.

'I thought maybe we'd start with the Torah blessings today,' I said. Jess screwed up her face, thrust her head forward and gave me a quizzical look while Darren mouthed the word 'what?' at me. I tipped my head almost imperceptibly towards Josh.

'Ok guys,' I said. 'Let's do these blessings together. Open up your folders and take out your sheets.' I saw Jess and Darren exchange confused looks and watched Jess jab her thumb in the direction of Josh, identifying him as the reason for this sudden change in format of these *bar-/bat-mitzvah* lessons. Josh still lay on his back, knees slightly bent, sheet of paper already in both hands, held out above his face.

'Darren, start us off please.' I didn't dare look into Darren's eyes – I didn't want to face his unasked question, which would have said 'Why are we doing this? What happened to all the interesting stuff?' I heard him say 'What?' in a grumpy tone. 'Read the first of the blessings please,' I said.

'What? *Bar'chu et Adonai ha-m'vorach*?' he asked in that same tone.

'That's the one,' I said. 'And we all respond *baruch Adonai ha-m'vorach l'olam va-ed.*'

I conducted their response with exaggerated waving arms – everyone joined in except Josh, who stared blankly at his sheet of paper, chewing frantically. 'Jess,' I said. She looked at me with a face that said 'What?' and I nodded at the sheet in her hand. 'Next one please.'

She tossed her hair, and then chanted: '*Baruch atah Adonai eloheinu melech ha-olam asher bachar banu mi-kol ha-amim v'natan lanu et torato, baruch atah Adonai notein ha-Torah.*' 'Very good,' I approved. 'Nice voice.' She smiled, but I could tell she was uncomfortable. There was a real atmosphere building up here.

'Josh?' I said.

'What?'

'Next blessing please.'

'What?'

'Read it. Please.' I saw Jess and Darren exchange another look, Jess shaking her head with exasperation. Alison was staring at the ground as ever.

The next bit happened really fast. From his prone position, Josh sprang up and stood looking down at me, screaming. 'I hate this Hebrew shit!' he shrieked and ran off in the direction of the auditorium. I rolled my eyes at Jess, Darren and Alison, all of whom looked shocked. 'Just start the DVD and watch it please guys,' I said, rising to my feet. 'I'll be back as soon as I can.'

I saw Darren lean forward and press the space bar on my laptop as I was moving away. Josh was seated on one of the benches in the auditorium, three rows back. His hands were pressed against his eyes and his shoulders were shaking – I guessed he was crying. What was this all about?

He didn't look up but I saw him tense as I approached. What did he think I was going to do to him? Drag him physically back to where the others were? I glanced back to the tree and saw that they were looking at me. I pointed at the laptop, waving my finger at them. They turned around.

'What's the deal, Josh,' I said gently.

He didn't lift his head, so his voice was muffled as he said, 'I don't want to do this frigging *bar-mitzvah*. And you can't frigging well make me do it.' He moved his hands and looked up now, red, tear-stained eyes showing defiance.

'Fine,' I said, shrugging my shoulders and keeping my voice calm. 'If you don't want to do a *bar-mitzvah*, then you don't have to do a *bar-mitzvah*. I really don't care.'

His mouth dropped open and he looked at me wide-eyed. 'No one can make you do this thing Josh,' I continued. 'You don't have to. So if you don't want to, don't. It won't make any difference to me. Or to God,' I added, standing up. 'Now are you coming back to watch TV or are you just going to sit here like a jerk?' That last bit was a gamble but I figured it was worth it.

'Just – er – just give me a minute ...' he stammered.

'When you're ready,' I said, making my way down the steps of the auditorium. I didn't look back. The other three quickly turned their heads back to look at the laptop, pretending they hadn't been watching us.

I didn't look back until I was sitting under the tree. The laptop screen was showing a picture of a man standing over a boy who was tied up on a pile of stones. The man was holding a knife and seemed about to kill the boy.

'What happened?' whispered Jess, turning to look at me.

'Sshhh,' I said, pointing at the laptop. I was smiling and both she and Darren saw me wink. 'Do not raise your hand against the child or do him any harm' said the laptop in a booming voice. The shot of the man and boy had pulled back to reveal an angel. The story of the *akedah*, the binding of Isaac, came to its conclusion when a ram was sacrificed in place of Abraham's son and I snapped the laptop shut. It occurred to me that I might have to cut out some of this lesson.

I saw Jess and Darren gesture at each other and in the direction of the auditorium with their eyes and I gave them both a fierce glare, designed to tell them to watch me and not look at the returning Josh. 'So what was that story all about?' I said, trying to sound as natural as I could. 'Don't look,' I hissed, as Josh approached slowly.

'Er … the binding of Isaac,' said Darren, trying to play his part.

'That's right,' I said, nodding as Josh lowered himself to the ground a short distance away, trying to remain as inconspicuous as possible. 'What do you think Abraham was <u>doing</u>?' I said, emphasising the word 'doing'. I gave Josh the slightest of nods, acknowledging his return to the group. He was sitting upright now.

'Well, God told him to kill his son, so he went right ahead and got ready to do it,' said Jess in a tone suggesting that God had asked Abraham to take Isaac to the movies.

'Don't you think that's just a teeny weeny bit crazy?' I asked.

'It's nuts.' Josh had made a contribution!

Trying not to sound over-enthusiastic, I asked 'Why do you think it's nuts, Josh?'

'It just is,' he said. 'I mean, why would God ask someone to kill their kid?' He still sounded angry.

'That's an important question,' I said, talking to the whole group now. ' Remember what we talked about yesterday,' I continued, avoiding eye contact with Josh, who hadn't been there yesterday. 'There is always some truth at the heart of these stories.'

'Yeah, but this is different,' protested Darren. 'Yesterday we talked about a story that had been built around a flood – a real event, told in a way to teach people a lesson. This is about one crazy man almost killing his poor kid! What lesson is that supposed to teach?'

'Don't kill your kid!' shouted Josh and we all laughed.

'Well, it's funny you should say that,' I said, after the laughter had died down. 'Take a look at Leviticus chapter 20.' I handed out the bibles. 'Who'd like to read it? Just the first three verses.'

Jess did her curtain-raising shake of her hair, then read: 'And the LORD spoke to Moses saying, "Say further to the Israelite people: 'Anyone among the Israelites or among the strangers residing in Israel who gives any of his offspring to Molech, shall be put to death: the people of the land shall pelt him with stones. And I will set My face against that man and will cut him off from among his people, because he gave of his offspring to Molech and so defiled My sanctuary and profaned My holy name.'" Jess looked up. 'What is that about?' she squealed.

I waited to see if any of them got it, but no one spoke. 'Molech was a Canaanite god,' I said, 'and the way people worshipped him was by giving him their children. Any idea how they did it?' All four shook their heads. 'They threw them into a huge fire,' I said, trying to sound like the voice that did the trailers for horror films.

'That's awful,' said Alison. The others nodded their agreement.

'But true,' I said. 'And the Israelites liked copying what the Canaanites did. Let's take a quick look at the book of Jeremiah.' Much flicking of pages as they all searched. 'Chapter 7, verses 30 and 31,' I added, then read:

'"For the people of Judah have done what displeases me," declares the LORD[9]. "They have set up their abominations in the House which is called by My name and have defiled it. And they have built the shrines of Topheth in the valley of Ben-Hinnom, to burn their sons and daughters in fire – which I never commanded, which never came to My mind."'

Darren looked up at me, waiting for an explanation. 'Okay,' I said. 'What do we learn from these words of Jeremiah?'

'That the people of Judah killed their own children?' asked Alison. It was good to see her getting more involved.

'Exactly,' I said. 'Even though the laws of Leviticus told them not to.' I tapped the bible lying on the ground in front of me.

'But God told Abraham to kill his son!' protested Jess. 'Why can't God make his mind up?' The others laughed but Jess looked really annoyed.

'Yes, but what was the outcome of that story?' I asked. 'Did Abraham kill Isaac?' They all shook their heads. 'So what point was the story trying to make?' There was a pause and then Alison said uncertainly 'That people shouldn't kill their children?'

---

[9] See note 4 p.20

'Right!' I said. 'But we know from what Jeremiah said that people were killing their children – throwing them into the fire.'

'That's disgusting,' said Jess, screwing up her face.

'But it happened,' I continued. 'And Jeremiah lived more than a thousand years after Abraham. So this crazy, disgusting thing was happening regularly.' I looked at each of them in turn. It seemed I had their attention - even Josh was still sitting upright.

'So what was the Abraham story trying to teach?' I said it slowly, trying to get them to see. It was Alison who got there first. 'That God didn't want the people to kill their children?' she asked, tentatively.

'That's it!' I exclaimed. 'The story was about someone who thought God wanted him to give his child as a sacrifice but he was told by God that this wasn't what God wanted and that a ram should be offered instead.'

'Poor ram,' said Jess, making a sad face. 'What did it do?'

'Shut up Jess,' said Josh, playfully.

'Killing a ram was a better idea than killing a human. Especially Isaac,' I added. 'Who was Isaac's most important son?'

'Jacob,' replied Darren.

'And if Isaac gets killed, no Jacob,' I continued. 'And no Jacob means no children of Israel, which means no us.' I opened my arms, indicating the four of them and the whole of the camp around us. 'So that story is saying "Listen you morons, don't kill your kids. Abraham didn't do it – and if he had, you wouldn't be here. So DON'T KILL YOUR CHILDREN. "'

Each of those four words was accompanied by a thump of my closed fist on the bible in front of me.

'So whenever you hear a story in the Torah, you need to ask yourself "What was this trying to tell the people who were listening to it? ". Sometimes, of course, it wasn't trying to tell them anything, it was only a source of entertainment. Let's have a quick look at one of those, the story of the meeting of Isaac and Rebekah. It's a good old-fashioned love story.'

They turned to the final verses of chapter 24 of Genesis. I quickly recounted the tale of how Abraham sent his servant to find a wife for his son and how he asked for God's help in choosing the right woman. Then he brought Rebekah back and she saw Isaac in the field doing whatever that strange thing was that he was doing in verse 63 of chapter 24. The verb is *la'su'ach*, which is translated as 'walking' or 'meditating,' but as it's the only time that word appears in the entire bible (I told them that was something called a *hapax legomenon*, but they weren't interested) no one actually knows what it means. Rebekah sees Isaac doing this thing and, according to all our English translations, she steps down from the camel on which she is riding (another crazy thing because we know that camels weren't around in that part of the Middle East until several hundred years after the patriarchs lived). But the Hebrew word for the way Rebekah gets down from her camel is *va-tipol*. And that word can only mean

one thing. She didn't step down or alight. She fell off. So when you put it all together, I told my amused little audience, the first time Rebekah sees Isaac, he's doing some unknown thing in the middle of a field and as a result of this, she falls off a non-existent camel. I tried to impress upon my young audience that this was meant to be an entertaining story – and how we had completely lost the fun of it because our tradition had turned it into something serious – which it was never meant to be.

'Of course some parts of the Torah are serious,' I said, 'but some aren't. And we need to be able to tell the difference.'

'Which brings me to another brilliant story,' I announced. 'We're running out of time, so we need to do this one quickly. It's another Genesis story you all know so well that you could probably sing it to me. "Way, way back many centuries ago …"' I sang. Alison and Darren joined in '"…not long after the bible began!"' and we all started laughing. There followed a brief resumé of the Joseph story, incorporating excerpts from the "Technicolour Dreamcoat" at suitable moments. I did have the DVD to hand but there wasn't much time left and, besides, we were doing a pretty good job ourselves. It reinforced my point about these stories etching themselves in our minds.

After several minutes of storytelling (which was each of the four trying to out-shout the others with episodes of Joseph's life while I tried to keep the story – and the storytellers – in order) we reached the finale, a rousing, tuneless chorus of "Any Dream Will Do". All five of us extended our arms and missed the final note by several miles before falling to the ground laughing. I was pleased to note that Josh seemed to be having as much fun as everyone else.

'Okay, now the serious bit,' I said, sitting up again and leaning against the tree once more. I ignored their groans and continued. 'What's the next thing we have to ask ourselves?'

'Can we sing "Jesus Christ Superstar"?' shouted Josh.

'Not today, Josh,' I said with mock severity. 'On Sunday maybe,' I added, with a smile. He laughed and I could sense everyone felt good. This, it seemed to me, was how teaching about Torah was meant to be.

'No, come on. We don't have long.' They didn't seem to be in the mood for serious thought any more and, to be fair to them, the purpose of this story wasn't as clear cut as the ones we'd looked at before. So I explained to them that the names of Jacob's twelve sons were those of the Israelite tribes and that they weren't all sons of one man all born in one generation. They were twelve tribal groups spread out across a large area of what would eventually become the kingdom of Israel, and across several centuries. There was no time to explain that their relative ages indicated their length of occupation of a particular part of the land (Reuben had been around the longest, Benjamin was a late arrival) or that the degree of emphasis a particular tribe had in the text indicated its prominence (especially Joseph's younger son Ephraim and his rival Judah). All there was time to do was to make a very simple point.

'The book of Genesis ends with the death of Jacob,' I said. 'What comes next?'

'Exodus,' said Darren quickly.

'Right. And where does that happen?'

'In Egypt,' said Alison. She and Darren were beginning to compete, I noticed.

'And where was Jacob when the story started?'

'Canaan' they both said together. Jess and Josh watched the competition silently.

'Exactly,' I said. 'And the whole purpose of the Joseph story is to create one very simple fact. In order for the Exodus to be able to take place, Jacob's descendants had to be in Egypt. So the last section of the book of Genesis gets them there. And wasn't it fun? Now go away.'

And they did. And they were smiling. Including Josh.

The fifth encounter – Tuesday night

As I approached the tree for our midnight rendezvous, I felt sure that I could hear him humming the tune of 'Any Dream Will Do'. But by the time I got there, he was silent and I wondered if I had just imagined it.

'Wonderful stories!' he exclaimed as I reached the tree and lowered myself to rest against it. 'Amazing how many different ways there are of telling the same old tales,' he continued. 'Mind you, I still do not know who Isaac is – the one who made that woman fall off her camel.' He sounded very cheerful.

'That woman, as you call her, was Jacob's mother,' I protested. There was no response. 'And what does *la'su'ach* mean?' I asked. He just laughed aloud and changed the subject.

'We did well to get Josh back into the group,' he said.

'Getting him to read the Hebrew really did the trick!' I agreed, acknowledging that it had been his idea. 'I wonder who he'll blame for the fact that his Hebrew didn't improve while he was at camp?'

'I do not hold out much hope for the success of his *bar-mitzvah* ceremony if he runs screaming into the distance every time someone asks him to read Hebrew,' agreed the prophet. 'But he is back in the group – and he was enjoying the stories at the end.'

'There are plenty more that I didn't have time to tell,' I said. 'And I'm sure he'd have loved them.'

'I am listening,' he said. It seemed as though it was time for a bedtime story or two.

'I assume you heard the one about Balaam and his donkey?' I enquired. 'Tell me more,' was his response. Surely not? He must know about the soothsayer of neighbouring Moab who had been asked by the Moabite king to curse the Israelites? He hadn't. So I briefly told the story – particularly the bit I knew best, which was when an angel – invisible to Balaam but clearly seen by the donkey on which he was riding – stood before him, sword drawn, to block his way. The donkey refused to move forward for fear of the angel but Balaam beat his donkey. Then, in the words of the bible, God 'opened up the donkey's mouth', and she explained to Balaam why she could go no further. Then the angel became visible to Balaam as well and he realised his error. He explained that his mission was to curse the Israelites on behalf of King Balak and was told that he could only utter words that God told him to utter. The words he spoke – '*Mah tovu ohalecha Ya'akov, mishk'notecha Yisra'el* - How good are your tents, O Jacob, your dwelling places, O Israel,' now form the opening of many synagogue services.

How he laughed! 'So your worship begins with the words of a Moabite soothsayer?' he exclaimed. 'After we tried so hard to paint them as evil idolaters?'

'King David was descended from a Moabite woman,' I protested.

'Do not be ridiculous,' he said sternly.

'In the book of Ruth we are told that she, a Moabitess, married Boaz, and they produced Obed, the grandfather of David,' I said.

'In the book of Numbers, according to what you just told me,' he retorted haughtily, 'a donkey saw an angel and then had a conversation with the Moabite soothsayer on his back who didn't. Then he did, and he went on to say nice things about us even though he was supposed to curse us. You should not believe everything you read in the Bible you know – not even the bit you call the Torah.' He paused, then added as an afterthought, 'Even if you do precede it with words declaring that it is God's true teaching.'

He was teasing, but there was a sharp tone to what he was saying. I was embarrassed – I should have known that the book of Ruth was unlikely to contain much in the way of historical truth.

I moved on. I told him the story of how Shechem raped Jacob's only daughter, Dinah, and how two of Jacob's sons, Simeon and Levi, got revenge. They persuaded Shechem and all his men to circumcise themselves as a sign of being part of the Israelite clan – then murdered them while they were recuperating and too weak to fight back.

'Very pleasant,' was his response to that story. I had the sense that he was getting bored.

'What's the matter?' I asked, tentatively.

'I am weary,' he replied. 'I have lived through the reign of four kings, I have seen our neighbours destroyed and watched Jerusalem become desperate and corrupt.'

'Don't you feel encouraged by the fact that, almost three thousand years after you wrote your words and gave your speeches, there are people in places you could never have imagined, in a world you could never have foreseen, still looking to you for inspiration?' I asked.

The tree seemed to shake. 'All I see is frivolity,' he proclaimed. I had a sense of him standing in the Temple forecourt in Jerusalem, yelling his fury at the insincere worshippers before him, accusing them of oppressing the poor, demanding of them that they change their ways. 'The same hollow worship that I saw in my time; nothing has substance, everything is for effect and entertainment. And still there is poverty and still there is injustice. Still there are slaves in the dungeons – '

'And you think the Torah has nothing to say about such things?' I snapped. I was beginning to tire of his negativity. 'I agree, the point of our joint venture is to remind our students of the true purpose of religion and there is much to find fault with in the way it is practised both in your time and mine. But let's not dismiss it so hastily. For all its failings, it was still a worthy attempt to understand and address the problems of the world and provide direction for our ancestors as they struggled to find their way.'

'By telling them stories about talking donkeys and Aramean women falling off creatures that first became known in King Solomon's time?' he protested.

'It's supposed to be entertaining as well as instructive,' I said. He was the one who had given me that information - and he had even said how much he'd enjoyed the stories. 'But there's so much more in the Five Books of Moses –'

'The Five Books of who?' he demanded. I explained how Orthodox tradition held that Moses had received the entire text of the Torah on Mount Sinai.

'And clearly you don't believe that,' he replied. 'Is that what makes you a Liberal Jew?'

'Basically, that's it,' I said. 'We don't accept the Orthodox belief that God wrote the Torah that was given to Moses. We recognise the Torah as being the product of several generations of prophets and priests, lawmakers and storytellers – which is exactly what you have told me and what I'm trying to get my students to understand. Firstly we need to be clear that it isn't telling us historical truth – it's not even trying to. As we have already agreed, it's a record of our ancestors' attempts to give meaning and structure to their lives.' The branches of the tree murmured their approval.

'And you've also made clear to me that those attempts are sometimes built upon historical experiences – even if they do get a bit exaggerated in the telling – as happened with the Exodus from Egypt –'

'The what?' he interrupted in an angry tone.

'The Exodus from Egypt,' I repeated. Surely this wasn't another biblical story of which he had no knowledge? 'The single most formative moment in the history of the Jewish people,' I continued, conscious that I was sounding a little pompous. 'According to the story in the Torah, the Egyptians were struck by terrible plagues and God led the enslaved Israelites to freedom across the Red Sea and through the wilderness to the Promised Land.' I knew I had some difficulty believing this story – but at that moment I was having more trouble coming to terms with the fact that Isaiah seemed not to know anything about it.

'The Exodus from Egypt,' he said with deliberation. 'That means people leaving Egypt, I assume?' I nodded. 'That would be Egypt where the river Nile is, where there are always crops growing on fertile ground, the place where the people of my often parched land went for food whenever there was drought and famine?' He paused. 'In every second generation, people travelled from Judah to Egypt to get food for their starving families. And they came back. Leaving Egypt was a regular occurrence – every Israelite either did it or knew someone who had done it. And they all had their stories to tell.' He paused.

'Some were treated kindly by the Egyptians, others were not,' he continued. 'There are many tales of brutality and slavery – and I seem to recall hearing a story about one particular tribe returning from such an experience following a miraculous deliverance. It may have been a formative experience for that particular tribe,' he said, 'but it was hardly whatever you just called it – the single most formative event in the history of the Jewish people ...'

This was intriguing. It certainly fitted with some of the theories I had read about of the actual grain of truth that lay at the heart of the Exodus story – namely that something extraordinary had happened to a group of my enslaved ancestors. Whatever it was – and I had some pretty firm ideas about that, which I intended to put to my group the following day - the consequence of it was that those ancestors had discovered freedom and made it a central plank of the religion they established, the religion that would eventually become Judaism.

I was astonished that this extraordinary story was not known to Isaiah – but then it seemed that he hadn't even heard of Moses! My encounter with this prophet from the eighth century BCE was confirming the Liberal Jewish view that the Torah was compiled from a variety of sources. The key to appreciating its significance lay in understanding what had motivated those biblical authors to compile it – and there was no doubt that the Exodus from Egypt, celebrated every year in Jewish tradition, was a crucial part of the whole process. That was clearly the next topic that needed to be addressed.

* * * * * * * * * * * * *

This was an easy lesson to plan. Many years ago as part of my rabbinic training, I had been asked to research and write an essay entitled 'Did the Exodus Really Happen?'. Part of that research had uncovered a theory that the plagues had been a consequence of a volcanic eruption on the Mediterranean island of Thera. I had told the story so many times that I didn't even need to read up on it. The challenge was to present it in a way that reminded my students of the basic Exodus story as presented in the Torah and then ask them to compare it with the volcano theory. After that, the key element was to ask them to consider the real significance of the story, which wasn't the historical accuracy of the plagues, but the consequence of whatever had happened. And the consequence was that the Israelite people had gained their freedom and at the heart of the new religion they established was the requirement for all to enjoy freedom.

LESSON FIVE – Wednesday afternoon

'Let my people go!'

I didn't doubt that Josh would be there again, along with the other three. He seemed to have made himself part of the group, though I wondered what he would do with that anger about his forthcoming *bar-mitzvah* ceremony now that I seemed to have deflected it. What surprised me was the fact that he had brought someone with him.

'This is my bunk mate Eric,' he said. 'I told him that we had a really cool time in this class so he wanted to check it out.' Eric was slightly taller than Josh and more athletic looking. His cropped blond hair contrasted with Josh's darker curls but they dressed the same: baggy t-shirt, baggy shorts, baseball cap pointing backwards and huge trainers (which they called sneakers).

'Hi, Eric,' I said, trying to conceal my surprise. 'Welcome. When is your *bar-mitzvah* ceremony?'

'I'm not having one,' he replied. 'My parents don't believe in that stuff – we don't go to Temple or anything,' he said, with just a hint of defiance.

'So why are you here?' I asked.

'Josh said it was cool,' he replied, doubtfully.

'I mean at camp,' I explained.

'Oh, Josh said that was cool too – and he's right.' Eric smiled. 'The sports and stuff are awesome!' He and Josh shared a high five and I raised my eyes at Jess and shook my head. She laughed.

'Well, welcome Eric,' I said, nodding to him. 'Welcome all of you.' I nodded in turn to Darren, Alison, Josh and Jess. 'We're one bible short today, but I think we'll manage.' Next to me was a blank flipchart.

'Yesterday we got our ancestors, the children of Israel, down into Egypt,' I reminded them. 'Today we're going to go through what happened to them while they were there and then we'll get them out again.' Picking up a thick felt pen, I knelt down next to the flipchart and said 'Okay guys. Just call out some of the things you associate with the story of the Exodus from Egypt.'

The words came thick and fast, and I couldn't say for sure who was shouting what. I wrote it all down as neatly as I could. But when it all went quiet and I said, 'I think that just about covers it,' we were left with a list that included the following in a rather haphazard way:

SLAVERY – PHARAOH – MOSES – SALT WATER – LAMB'S BLOOD – RED SEA – PLAGUES (I'd put that at the top right hand corner and asked them to name the ten plagues, so underneath it were the following: BLOOD, FROGS, LOCUSTS, HAIL, DARKNESS, DEATH OF FIRSTBORN, LICE, WILD ANIMALS, BOILS, CATTLE DISEASE) – MATZAH – BITTER HERBS – EGG.

Moving the flipchart slightly to one side, I arranged it and myself so that we could both rest against the tree facing our audience. 'Okay, let's try and make some sense of this stuff,' I said. 'Listen up.'

'As we know, Jacob and his sons – even though we know they weren't really his sons as such – arrived in Egypt. Over a period of time they grew more numerous and the Pharaoh – the ruler of Egypt – made them work for him as slaves. Interestingly, we only know of him as Pharaoh, which just means 'ruler', the bible is careful not to tell us which Pharaoh it is.'

'I thought it was Rameses the Second?' said Darren. I was impressed.

'The only mention of Rameses is the name of one of the cities the Israelites built,' I replied. 'That doesn't mean that Rameses was the actual Pharaoh. Anyway, remember that the Exodus story, like all those Genesis accounts we looked at, was a story being told from generation to generation. And it may have changed a bit – well, quite a lot actually – as it passed from one generation to the next. And because the Pharaoh has no name, we have no idea when these events were supposed to have taken place.

'But let's stick with the story that we have in our biblical book of Exodus. The Israelites are slaves to the Egyptians. Moses, who escapes death when Pharaoh has all the baby boys killed, grows up in Pharaoh's palace, then runs away, only to return to be the leader who leads the Israelites to freedom. Along with his brother Aaron, Moses confronts Pharaoh. Each time he goes to him, he asks Pharaoh to let the Israelites go and threatens him with a plague if he doesn't. Pharaoh doesn't, the plague happens, Moses goes back and threatens him with the next plague – and so on, right up till the tenth and final plague.

'Let's put them in order by the way – here's how they occur in the book of Exodus: blood, frogs, lice, wild animals, cattle disease, boils, hail, locusts, darkness, death of the firstborn. After the final plague, Pharaoh relents and tells Moses to get out and take the people with him. But then Pharaoh changes his mind and chases after them. The Israelites – there are six hundred thousand men by the way – which would make at least two million people when you add women and children – get safely across the Red Sea, which has kindly parted to let them through. Then, just as the Egyptians follow, it closes again, drowning Pharaoh and all his army. The end. Great story, eh?' The audience nodded.

'But pretty gruesome, don't you think? A lot of suffering, a lot of violence. And it shows us a God who is quite happy to beat up one group of human beings – the Egyptians, while being kind to another – the Israelites. Why would God do that? And it gets worse. You probably heard the bit about Pharaoh hardening his heart and refusing to let the Israelites go? Near the climax of the story, there's a subtle change. Listen to this – just before the eighth plague: "And the Eternal One spoke to Moses and said 'Go to Pharaoh, for I have hardened his heart and the heart of his servants that I might show my signs before him so that you may tell your children and your children's children the things that I did among them and know that I am the Eternal One.' '''' [10]

'I have hardened Pharaoh's heart,' I repeated. 'Pharaoh doesn't have a choice. He can't let the people go, even if he wants to. Why? Because God wants to prove that he's more powerful. How crazy is that?' I looked around and they seemed to agree that it was crazy.

'When I was your age, I listened to that stuff and decided that I didn't like a God who behaved like a school bully and went round beating one lot of people up while showing favouritism to another group. I also didn't believe that the plagues happened that way anyway – it made no sense!' I remembered the Sunday morning classroom arguments with the Orthodox rabbi who assured me that if I didn't believe all this was true, then I wasn't really Jewish.

'So how come you're a rabbi?' asked Josh. 'I mean if you don't believe what's written in the Torah, doesn't that make it kinda hard?'

'Sometimes,' I conceded. 'But if I had to believe everything that's in the Torah, then I wouldn't even want to be a rabbi. I see it as my job to try and make sense of it; to understand why our ancestors wrote what they did, what they were trying to answer or explain and separate out the bits they got right from the bits that just don't work any more – though maybe they did in their world three thousand years ago. And I think it's important that you guys have a sense of that too if this *bar-/bat-mitzvah* thing – and Judaism as a whole – is going to have any meaning for you.'

I looked at each of them, trying to get a sense of whether my words were having any impact. Well, they were here, which was a good start, and they seemed to be listening. Of them all, Darren looked the most appreciative. It was hard to tell what was going on behind Alison's glasses, Jess seemed preoccupied with one of her fingernails, though it could have been her way of concentrating. Josh and Eric seemed to be following what was going on – I wondered if Eric would come back for more tomorrow? Meanwhile, I thought, let's get on with today. I loved this bit – it was this particular explanation of the Exodus that had brought me back to Judaism and given me my understanding of how this whole religion thing was meant to work. Let's see if I could do it for these guys too.

'So you can believe that everything happened just as it's written in the Torah,' I began, 'the plagues coming one after the other in a nice neat sequence after Moses had been to see Pharaoh, to be told the people would not be released. And then there's the numbers. Like I said before, the total number of people who left Egypt according to the Torah would have been more than two million. That's more than a quarter of the entire population of Egypt at the time. And as you may know from some of your school studies, the Egyptians were a very sophisticated society and they kept efficient records. You think they'd have made a note somewhere of a quarter of the population getting up and leaving one night?' They listened.

'Not a whisper,' I said, after what seemed a long enough pause for dramatic effect. 'And not only that, it's been worked out that if two million people marched six abreast in tight formation across the Sinai desert, the first ones would be arriving in Jerusalem at the same

---

[10] Exodus 10:1-2

time as the last ones were leaving Egypt. The numbers just don't add up,' I concluded, with an expansive spread of my arms.

'Another thing,' I added. 'We know that the land of Canaan, where our ancestors lived, was mostly desert and there was often a shortage of food.'

'We heard it in the Joseph story yesterday,' Josh interjected.

'That's good, Josh,' I said approvingly. 'And where did they go to find food?'

'Egypt!' said at least three of them.

'Exactly,' I continued. 'And there was probably a famine at least every fifty years or so, so every Canaanite would have in their experience at least one journey to Egypt – if not them, then a family member. And if you go down to Egypt, you have to come back – so everyone had a story about leaving Egypt – or knew someone who did.'

I looked around at my audience. 'Okay, let's remember what we learned about those Genesis stories we covered,' I said. 'Think of Noah's Ark, a crazy story, for sure, but there was a solid fact at the heart of it: a destructive flood. Now let's look at the Exodus story, with God doing magic tricks and behaving like a playground bully, and ask if maybe something real lay at the heart of that story too.' They watched.

'Okay, here goes. We know – again from archaeology – that there was a massive volcanic eruption on an island in the Mediterranean Sea at around the time the Israelites would have been in Egypt. It was massive – half an island just disappeared. It was called Thera - its modern name is Santorini. I went there once and you can see that half the island is just, well, missing. And the consequences of the eruption would have been felt in the Delta region of the Nile, on the opposite shore of the Mediterranean – again, archaeology has proved this.

'And the after effects of volcanic eruptions have been well-documented in other incidents. We know that, for example, the ash that comes out of a volcano is full of iron oxide – which is red and smells like blood because of the iron. It would have blown over from this volcano and landed in the rivers, turning them red. And if the river gets clogged with volcanic dust, those that live in it will die – but those that can get out …' I paused, inviting a little audience participation.

'Frogs!' cried Jess, excitedly.

'… do just that.' I concluded my sentence like we were acting out a pre-rehearsed script.

I went on, quickly now, explaining how swarms of insects travel away from an erupting volcano, and there was a period of darkness as the dust clouds gathered. The animal world was disrupted too: animals choking on the falling dust or stampeding in panic. As I offered an explanation for each of the plagues, I crossed them off my list.

'The hail is the most interesting,' I continued. 'The bible calls it "hail with fire flashing in it, the like of which has never been seen before. " If you've never seen molten lava falling from the sky, that's about the best way to describe it, I suppose. And if it landed on you,' I slapped myself on my bare arm, 'you'll get –'

'Boils!' That was Alison – she was really with us now. They all looked, well, kind of excited, like detectives successfully uncovering one clue after another that would answer a mysterious case.

I fed them another one. 'Now let's do the Red Sea,' I said. 'First of all, it's not the Red Sea – that's been wrongly translated into English. The Hebrew is *yam suf*, which means 'sea of reeds'. That's a marshy area just to the north east of the Delta region of the Nile, where the Israelites were. It was easy enough to cross if you were on foot but an army on horseback and in chariots had no chance. They'd get stuck in the mud. And while they were stuck, something happened that also often occurs after a volcanic eruption or an earthquake under the sea. We mentioned it a couple of days ago. Until recently you'd never have heard of it, but now –'

'Tsunami!' cried Eric. The rest nodded in recognition, recalling the horrific scenes of the Asian disaster the previous December.

'Yep!' I agreed, nodding. 'After volcanic eruptions at sea, the water simply withdraws – leaving what had once been deep water as dry land for maybe two or three days. Then – bang! – back it comes in a great wave – a tsunami. Bye-bye Pharaoh, bye-bye Egyptians.'

I paused, enjoying the thoughtful expressions on all of their faces. Alison seemed to be the most animated. She was the one who spoke first. 'What about the tenth plague?' she asked. 'You can't tell me that a volcano goes around just killing first born children and noticing those houses that have a mark on their doorposts,' she challenged.

'Good point,' I said. 'This is where I need you to do some thinking. Remember what we said about Hurricane Katrina – or Noah's flood? How people often believed that a natural disaster was because the god or gods they believed in were angry with them?' Those who recalled the discussions nodded.

'Well, that's what the Egyptians thought. So they did all their religious stuff, trying to make their god like them again – and none of it worked. The bad stuff just kept happening – not in sequence like in our Exodus story, but all in one go. And eventually it must have occurred to them that maybe it wasn't their gods who were angry – perhaps it was the god of the people they had enslaved. So they went and asked the Canaanite slaves what they did when their god was mad at them. And what answer do you think they got – remember the Abraham and Isaac story from yesterday?'

'Oh my God,' said Darren, as a light seemed to go on in his head. 'They sacrificed their firstborn,' he continued in an awestruck voice, gently shaking his head as he spoke.

'Exactly,' I went on. 'So the Egyptian guy takes this news back to Pharaoh who says "Blimey! That's a bit extreme!" but realises that the situation he and his people are in calls for extreme measures. And so a decree goes out, that everyone is to kill everything that is firstborn: whether it be child, calf or any other animal. And one group of people, who had been slaves for years, said "No way!" and decided to run away that night. And those people,' I said with a final grand flourish of my arms, 'were our ancestors, the children of Israel. They escaped into the wilderness, into freedom, and carried with them this story of extraordinary events. And we all know what happens with stories of extraordinary events …' I said.

'They get exaggerated,' said Jess, with a smile.

'They sure do,' I said. 'And this one was pretty big to start with. To those who were there, it must indeed have seemed like God was battering the Egyptians and giving the slaves a chance to escape. That story was told and re-told – usually at times when the people would gather together for big celebrations – like the spring festival, which we'll talk more about another time. It was at least five hundred years between the events happening and them finally being written down – imagine how much the story grew in that time. All the events that had happened simultaneously were separated by Moses going to visit Pharaoh, just to make the story longer and more exciting to listen to. And those events made such an impression on the people who experienced them and on those who heard the story that they based their whole religion around its message. They believed that what happened to Pharaoh was punishment for having made the Israelites slaves. So over and over again we hear in the Torah that the Israelites should not oppress strangers because they knew what it was like to be oppressed strangers in Egypt. You know what it was like, so don't do it to anyone else.

'And that, ladies and gentlemen, is the story of the Exodus – or should I say, one alternative version of it. In the end, we live in a free society and no one can tell us what we have to believe. So you're free to choose whether you want to believe in a God who behaves like the one in the book of Exodus – rescuing a group of people he likes and punishing the group of people he doesn't like because they were cruel to them – and seriously messing around with nature in the process. Or you can believe that a frightened group of slaves suddenly saw an opportunity to get themselves and their families out of slavery because of the chaos that is caused by a natural event. Somehow they found the courage to run away – and they found freedom as a result. Where does God fit into that? Maybe God works in human life by giving us courage to take advantage of such situations. I know which God I believe in, I know which one works for me. You make your choice – that's what this *bar-/bat-mitzvah* thing is <u>really</u> all about.'

There was a pause and I added a final thought. 'I always get myself into trouble when I tell this version of the story – it's like people think I'm trying to disprove it. But I'm not, I'm really not. What I'm doing is rescuing it from being something improbable and frankly unbelievable and making it possible. When I was the same age as you guys, I walked away from Judaism because my rabbi – an Orthodox rabbi – insisted that I had to believe that what was described in the Torah really happened. And I couldn't get my head round a God who behaves with such cruelty. But this version works for me: it's about a people – *my* people – taking advantage of some extraordinary happenings to free themselves from slavery – and then build a whole religion based on the concept that God wants us to have freedom and justice. And that's why the twelve-year-old me who didn't believe what was written in the Torah is teaching you about it as a rabbi now.'

'Awesome, man!' said Eric. I wasn't sure if it was to Josh or to me. Darren actually clapped twice before stopping, realising that maybe that wasn't an appropriate response.

'Way to go, Rabbi,' said Jess, rising to her feet. Or maybe she said 'I have to go, Rabbi,' as she had seen one of her friends walk past and figured it was okay to leave. Well, I was done. Almost …

'One last thing,' I said. 'We know that the people leaving Egypt would have been able to see the volcano on the horizon as they left. Anyone know how the bible describes how God led them through the wilderness?'

'A pillar of fire,' Darren began, then faded out.

'By night,' I continued, 'and –'

'– a pillar of cloud by day,' concluded Alison.

I smiled to my little group as if to say 'you choose' as they gathered their folders and headed thoughtfully to their cabins.

TISH'AH B'AV

The lights of the candles flickered, looking fragile and vulnerable in the evening breeze. Hundreds of Jewish children sat facing the stage of this large outdoor auditorium, listening to readings that commemorated this fateful evening of the ninth of Av. They huddled together, for warmth, or perhaps for comfort, as young voices recounted tales of different times and different places when Jews had huddled together.

This was the camp's observance of *Tish'ah b'Av*, the anniversary of the destruction of the first Jerusalem Temple by the Babylonians in 586 BCE, the second Jerusalem Temple by the Romans more than six hundred and fifty years later, and the cruel treatment suffered by the Jews in so many lands through the Middle Ages and beyond. It seemed appropriate that one of the few European participants at this North American Jewish summer camp had been given the role of selecting and co-ordinating the readings for this ceremony. Young voices pierced the night air, reminding this latest generation of Jews of the suffering of those who had come before them. Would this observance remind these privileged youngsters of their obligations to those who preceded them? Would they appreciate their duty to keep this ancient faith and pass it on to those who would follow? That was the question the flickering candles seemed to ask as the stories of brutality and pain filled the chill of the Californian evening.

JERUSALEM 70 CE

'See how the Temple burns! How can this be happening to us again? We remember how the Babylonians destroyed the Temple of King Solomon over six hundred and fifty years ago and see this horror repeated before our eyes. See the flames climbing into the sky! Listen to the screams of the women watching their children being carried away by the Roman soldiers.

'Look at the soldiers coming out of the doors of the burning Temple, carrying its treasures – God's treasures – stealing from the House of the Eternal. How will our religion survive now that this horror is happening to us? I am a priest of the House of God but if I have no Temple in which to serve, how then can our God be praised? Is there no hope, no possibility that Judaism has a future?

'I have heard that our burning Temple will be replaced by other houses of prayer, buildings known as synagogues. I have heard that a great teacher of our religion, a Rabbi named Yochanan ben Zakkai, has been given permission by the Roman emperor to establish a house of learning at a place called Yavneh. Perhaps this great and learned man will be able to keep Judaism alive. But for now all I can do is watch as God's Temple is burned to the ground, watch as the Roman soldiers steal the gold from God's house, stand here defiantly as another Roman soldier approaches me, his sword drawn and ready to kill …

SOUTHEND, ENGLAND 1290 CE

'This is a terrible day. King Edward the Second, the King of England, has declared that we must leave his country. My family has been here for over two hundred years and during that time we became very wealthy and lived in the house that my grandfather built in the city of Lincoln. But on July 18ᵗʰ in this year, the year 1290, the King issued a decree that all Jews must leave England – and must leave all their possessions and money behind. This is a sad day in Jewish history – it is the ninth day of the month of Av, the day when we recall the destruction of the Temple in Jerusalem. And now we have *another terrible event to recall on this day.*

'Over there is my family and hundreds of other people from the city of Lincoln. The ship on which we were travelling is stuck on sandbanks and so the captain told us to get off the ship and to take a walk to stretch our legs until the tide came in and the ship could refloat itself. The tide is coming in now – it is already around my ankles – so I shall gather my family and return to the ship. But I see there is some commotion – my fellow Jews are trying to get on board the ship but the captain has removed the ropes. He is laughing and shouting – I must get closer so that I can hear what he is saying.

'He says, "Come on you Jews! Pray to your leader Moses that he will once again turn the sea into dry land for you!" And he is laughing. His sailors are standing at the side of the ship and laughing too, spitting on us, waving at us, mocking us as the sea climbs higher. We will not be allowed back on his ship. We are going to drown here at the coast of England, this country which has expelled us. My children, my wife, my family and I – we are all going to drown.'

RAVENSBURG, GERMANY 1431 CE

From an official church decree dated 27ᵗʰ July 1431: The parishioners of the community of Ravensburg have for some months now been desperately anxious regarding the disappearance of young Hans Wintermeier, the son of Friedrich, the miller of our town. Since the ten-year-old boy's disappearance shortly before Holy Week, our suspicions have fallen upon the Jews of Ravensburg but we have not been able to establish any proof.

Now we can tell you with absolute certainty that young Hans was indeed the victim of ritual murder by the Jews of this town. The ten-year-old boy's body was found dumped in a nearby forest and it was clear from the wounds which had been inflicted upon the poor little angel that all of his blood had been drained from his body. This can only mean one thing: that the evil Jews have once again engaged in their appalling custom of using the blood of a Christian child to prepare the unleavened bread for their devilish Passover celebrations.

Accordingly the upstanding Christian citizens of Ravensburg are instructed, in the name of their religion, to enter the Jewish part of the town and exact revenge for the tragic murder of young Hans Wintermeier. Permission is given for you to destroy the property of the Jews, to demand that they accept our Lord as their true Saviour and, should they refuse this offer of redemption, to dispatch their souls to heaven where they may meet their final judgment.

The Ecclesiastical Authorities of Ravensburg

GRANADA, SPAIN July 31ˢᵗ 1492 CE

To the person who reads this letter:

I do not know to whom, I am addressing this letter. I do not even know if anyone will ever read it. I am writing it in the cellar of my house in the Spanish city of Granada. I have been living here with my family for a week now, hiding from the Cardinals and the Inquisitors who have been patrolling the streets of this city seeking out the Jews from their homes.

The King and Queen of Spain, Ferdinand and Isabella, have issued a decree saying that all Jews must leave the country by today. Today is Tishah b'Av, the day when we remember the destruction of the Temple in Jerusalem. And today is the day when I must pretend to stop being a Jew, act as though I am a Christian because any Jew found in this country after today will be tortured and forced to convert to Christianity or be put to death.

And so I write this letter. I hope that the person who reads it will do so in freedom, in a place where people are free to practise their religion, to believe in the God they want to believe in. And I hope that in that place, Judaism will be one of the religions which will still be alive. Who knows? Perhaps even you, the person reading my letter, are Jewish … If that is so, then please remember me on Tishah b'Av, remember how I was forced to pretend that I wasn't Jewish and be grateful for the opportunity you have to celebrate your religion. May God protect you and may you live in safety.

Julietta Mendes da Costa

LVOV, UKRAINE August 1648 CE

In the year 1648 in the area of Europe now known as the Ukraine, Cossack soldiers went on the rampage in villages and towns. This is an account from a Lithuanian Rabbi Shabbetai ben Meir HaCohen (1621-1662) also known as the Shach, who survived this time:

'On the same day 1,500 people were killed in the city of Human in Russia on the Sabbath. The nobles [Cossacks], with whom the wicked mob had again made an alliance, chased all the Jews from the city into the fields and vineyards where the villains surrounded them in a circle, stripped them to their skin and ordered them to lie on the ground. The villains spoke to the Jews with friendly and consoling words: "Why do you want to be killed, strangled and slaughtered like an offering to your God Who poured out His anger upon you without mercy? Would it not be safer for you to worship our gods, our images and crosses and we would form one people which would unite together." But the holy and faithful people who so often allowed themselves to be murdered for the sake of the Lord, raised their voices together to the almighty in Heaven and cried: "Hear O Israel the Lord our God, the Holy One and the King of the Universe, we have been murdered for Thy sake so often already. O Lord God of Israel let us remain faithful to Thee." Afterward they recited the confession of sins and said: "We are guilty and thus recognise the Divine judgement"' Now the villains turned upon them and there was not one of them who did not fall victim.'

It's no wonder when Jews hear the word Cossack they break out in a sweat. These people killed 100,000 Jews and destroyed 300 Jewish communities in the most brutal way one could imagine.

Yet to this day Chmielnicki is considered a nationalist hero in the Ukraine, where they regard him as a kind of 'George Washington'. In Kiev there is a big statue in the square erected in his honour.

The silent audience rose, numbed, perhaps by the evening's chill, perhaps by the horror of the suffering of their ancestors about which they had just heard. A rabbi from England, took the microphone and read the evening's final prayers:

On this ancient day of mourning, we weep for a hundred generations of our victims and martyrs who have suffered and perished because of the cruelty of their fellow human beings. Their blood still cries out to us from all the corners of the earth: from Jerusalem, from England, from Spain, from Russia, from Auschwitz.

A voice is heard in Ramah, lamentation and bitter weeping! Rachel is weeping for her children, refusing to be comforted for her children, for they are no more.

But there is hope. There is hope because even in times of deepest darkness, there was courage, compassion and decency; the human spirit was not entirely defeated, and a remnant of our people survived. There is hope because, powerful though the forces of evil are, the forces of good are mightier still. There is hope because of our belief that God's purpose will, in the end, be fulfilled. There is hope because of our faith that, at some future time, human beings will respond to the good within them and the God beyond them and, as partners with God, will usher in that longed-for age of love and amity, friendship and peace, for us and all peoples.

The hope of the Prophets, which has become the hope of Judaism, issues from the faith in God's concern for this world ... The moral law, which rules history, assures that ultimately the world will be changed into the better world which God's rule requires.

Following the recital of the *Kaddish*, guitar chords cut through the darkness and words of Israel's ancient prophets were sung, as if in defiance at the stories that had been told:

> A day will dawn in a time to come
> A day when God's name shall be One
> All war and suffering shall be through
> When that day comes – *ba-yom ha-hu*

> > *Ba-yom ha-hu* and on that day
> > I will wipe all tears away
> > Sorrow and pain shall all be gone
> > And My name it shall be One
> > *Ba-yom ha-hu, ba-yom ha-hu*

> Let justice and righteousness flow like a stream
> The old and the young shall see visions and dream
> And what we dream shall yet come true
> When that day comes - *ba-yom ha-hu*

> They shall not hurt or destroy in Your holy place
> Your word shall be known to the whole human race
> On their lips, in their hearts so they'll know what to do
> When that day comes - *ba-yom ha-hu*

The spear will break and the chariot burn
The hearts of the parents to children will turn
And children to parents - and all turn to You
When that day comes - *ba-yom ha-hu*

The sixth encounter – Wednesday night

I could feel his sadness and his pain that night when I was still a long distance from the tree. Or maybe it was mine. But it was both strange and fitting to be sharing that pain across so many centuries of Jewish suffering. I felt the bark of the tree dig into me as I sat myself down and wanted it to hurt.

'Oh my God,' he said. I silently mused that this was the same phrase that Jess might use on breaking a fingernail. 'So these are the things that await my people?' he continued, in a whisper. It was phrased as a question, but I don't think he expected a reply from me.

We shared a long silence, each trying, I suppose, to make sense of the events of the centuries that separated our lives and the suffering of the people whose identity united us. I couldn't, and I didn't suppose he could either.

'*Lo yisa goy el goy cherev, v'lo yil'm'du od milchamah,*' I said. It felt strange to be quoting him back at himself. 'Nation shall not lift up sword against nation, neither shall they learn war any more.'

'What is that?' he asked softly.

'Words of yours,' I replied, surprised that he didn't seem to recognise them. 'Your vision that all weapons of war shall be made into ploughshares and pruning hooks and that no human will ever kill another again.' He said nothing. 'Those words are outside the United Nations building in New York,' I continued, 'the organisation that, in theory at least, is supposed to try and make that happen, nearly three thousand years after you wrote those words. And it still hasn't happened ...'

'Those were Micah's words,' he said, after a long pause, 'and they became part of our Jerusalem tradition.' I gave a silent laugh that was just an exhalation of breath.

'Well the world has given them to you,' I said.

'A pity the world hasn't taken any notice of them, whoever's words they are,' he said sadly.

'All that hatred, all that killing, all that suffering,' he cried. And he was crying, I had no doubt of that. 'How can this happen? How can the Eternal One let this happen?'

'I was hoping you would be able to tell me that ...' I said.

'What is there to tell?' he replied. 'This is the work of humanity, not the work of God. We are given the tools, the skills and the knowledge – and we use it to find ways to kill and maim, to hurt and destroy. The way is laid out for us, the path is shown to us but we choose not to follow it and walk in ways of wickedness. Aiiiiiieeee!'

The sound of his wailing cut through me, piercing my very soul, or so it felt. It seemed to encapsulate the anguish and bewilderment, the hurt and the incomprehension with which countless Jews had been forced to confront their premature deaths across so many centuries.

'And so much of this because one group of people developed a different understanding of God from another,' he eventually said, after another mournful silence. 'And they used some of your words to justify themselves,' I added, shaking my head at the cruel irony. 'And yet these people have remained faithful to their God, to their heritage for all this time, despite the suffering that was visited upon them. For more time than I had ever imagined was possible, in more places and more ways than I had ever dreamed of, through more pain and more suffering than I could have envisioned. Does this not in some way talk to us of the power of Israel's God, of the Torah of *YHWH*, the instructions of the Eternal One that my fellow prophets and I sought to impart? And how important those words are – and how they are ignored!'

There was a silence which echoes of the evening's readings seemed to fill. I clenched my fists in rage at the insanity of this world which could have been so good but which persisted in tearing itself apart on the basis of divisions and misunderstandings between the humans who dwelt on it. Eventually my anger burned itself out. I wondered if he was still there, or if he had chosen to have nothing more to do with this twenty-first century, just as it seemed to have chosen to have nothing more to do with him and his visions of justice and peace.

'Say something,' I pleaded, after what might have been as much as five minutes of silence. I needed him to validate the choice of all those countless millions of my ancestors who had died in the name of the faith of which he was one of the guiding lights.

'Please!' I pleaded. 'Help me find comfort. Understanding.' I placed my head in my hands, resting my elbows on my knees and stared at the dark ground beneath me. 'Remember your words: *u-m'chah YHWH dim'ah me'al kol panim, v'yasu yagon v'anachah'* 'And the Eternal One will wipe away the tears from every face, sorrow and sighing shall flee away.' I knew those words from the funeral service, and had incorporated them in the chorus of my song – they always helped me to realise that the resilience of the human spirit somehow enables human beings to overcome even the most overwhelming of tragedies.

'Those lines go well together,' he said in a thoughtful tone. I extended my arms in a shrug to the heavens and, lifting my head, rolled my eyes disbelievingly in the same direction. Here we were reflecting on human barbarity to countless generations of Jews through the ages, and all he could do was consider a new combination of some of his lyrics. Whatever. Maybe that was his way of saying that there was no point in trying to analyse this mess. What was important was to try and shine a light to help find a way out of it, and if words could provide that light then they needed to be good and to inspire.

'So now you see why the task of teaching understanding is so important,' he declared. 'There is nothing to be gained only by repeating knowledge. True wisdom comes only when there is understanding. And true understanding comes only when people learn what it is that God requires of them: to do justly, love mercy and to walk humbly with their God.'

'Isn't that another one of Micah's?' I asked, recognising the well-known passage in which the prophet Micah also spoke out against the bullocks that were being offered in the Temple.

'We all worked on those words together,' he replied dismissively. 'A group of us used some standard phrases and images to make our point to the people of Jerusalem – who rarely listened.' He paused. 'That song at the end of the service. I recognised some of the lines as being similar to mine – they shall not hurt or destroy in Your holy place.

But there were some other lines in that final song that were new to me – and most impressive. What was their source?'

I explained that I had compiled the lyrics of the song *Ba-yom ha-hu* from different statements by various prophets; their visions for the messianic age of peace which it was the duty of humankind to work to implement. I mentioned the names of Elijah, Amos, Joel and Zechariah, informing him that the last of those was the author of the words on which the song was based.

'*Ba-yom ha-hu yih'yeh YHWH echad u-sh'mo echad,*' he recited. '"On that day the name of the Eternal shall be One and known to be One." Having listened to this evening's readings, that seems a distant dream.'

'But we have to keep dreaming it!' I protested, angry at the defeatism in his voice. 'We cannot – must not – despair. We must work to maintain your dream, to keep God – and your vision of God – in our world!'

'The face of the Eternal One is often hidden from us,' he mused. 'And the voice of the Divine can be difficult to hear. But we must listen out for God's voice, search for God's presence in order to gain the knowledge and understanding that we need to keep alive the vision of a better world, a world in harmony with itself and its creator. Such a world will not contain the sad stories of which we heard this night of *Tisha'ah to Tish' ah,*' he concluded. 'And each of us can find God and keep that vision, that dream alive.'

'How do we find it?' I asked quietly. 'How does an awareness of God, of the divine influence on our lives as individuals and societies, find its way into our consciousness?'

'A crucial question,' he agreed. 'Does God speak to us through blinding revelations and miraculous manifestations? Sometimes, perhaps,' he conceded thoughtfully, as though recalling an encounter of his own.

'But there is something of the divine implanted in each of us,' he continued. 'Our task is to search for it, find it and incorporate it in our lives, wherever and whenever we happen to live. It is that within us that encourages us to search for meaning and purpose in our lives, to strive to progress, to develop a civilisation where the brutality and hatred that are also part of our nature will ultimately be overcome by our potential to be good.

'All around us and within us are silent indicators, pointing us towards that ultimate human destination. But it is up to us to search for them, listen to them and act upon them. That is the true purpose of religion, the reason why we engage in the quest for meaning. The tragic events about which you read this evening are the consequence of our failure to recognise this simple truth.'

Countless stars blinked in the dark, cloudless sky, as though beaming an urgent message in an unknown code to a silent planet below.

* * * * * * * * * * * *

61

I walked slowly back to my cabin. Above me the moon shone brightly, surrounded by stars. I needed to think of a way to get my students to consider how the voice of God spoke to human beings. I didn't expect or want them to believe that it was through fiery displays of signs and wonders – I certainly didn't. But I wanted to get them to consider how we – all of us – might occasionally catch a glimpse of something beyond us or deep within us that might encourage or inspire us to take a step forwards in our lives; a step towards becoming what we had the potential to become.

I recalled a reading in the Liberal prayerbook that I had memorised because it had so moved me and was part of the inspiration that led me to embark on my journey towards becoming a rabbi. It went '… dimly we have seen a vision, faintly heard a voice not ours. The blazing stars, particles too small to see, the mind reaching out, the smile of children, the eyes of lovers, melody filling the soul, a flood of joy surprising the heart, a helping hand, the apprehension of mystery at the core of the simplest things – all these tell us that we are not alone. They reveal to us God, the vision that steadies and sustains us.'[11]

The question was how to put this across to a group of twelve-year-olds. I needed to find a way of getting them to think about the ways in which human beings are inspired to grow and make progress – and how we might define or describe that as 'God'. That prayer was a good start – and maybe I could get them to share their experiences of sudden inexplicable inspiration that might be called revelation. Of course, there were revelations in the bible – and I'd use those for sure – but I needed something else, a different perspective that my students could relate to. A memory of a favourite scene from a film I had seen in my childhood came into my mind. The film was '2001: A Space Odyssey'. Many years ago it had encouraged me to ask where inspiration came from, what was the source of human understanding and growth. I took one final glance at the stars before entering my cabin. The next day's lesson was already formed in my mind before I even sat down at my computer.

---

[11] Service of the Heart, ULPS, London 1967. p.93

LESSON SIX – Thursday afternoon

'Encountering God.'

It was a relief to be watching the DVD. Getting them to focus on the Sinai revelation in chapter 19 of Exodus had been a real struggle – and I couldn't quite work out why. Perhaps it was the residue of the sadness left over from the previous night's reflections on so much pain and suffering, perhaps it was because today was, after all, still *Tish'ah b'Av*, the saddest day in the Jewish calendar. It was a day for feeling sorry for oneself, that was for sure, but most people at this camp didn't need a special day set aside for that activity. Whatever it was, there was something affecting my little group.

It was a growing little group, however. It seemed that Eric had been sufficiently impressed by the retelling of the Exodus story to return with Josh for more today. And Jess, not to be outdone ('Well if he can bring a friend along then I don't see why I can't bring one too') was now accompanied by Julie, who, I had ascertained, was due to celebrate becoming *bat-mitzvah* the following January but whose parents had generously not required her to take lunchtime *bat-mitzvah* lessons. So here she was doing them voluntarily! I suppose I should have taken it as a compliment but I was worried that the dynamic of the group was being disrupted – Darren – and in particular Alison – seemed somewhat put out by this latest arrival. Maybe this change in dynamics was what was affecting their concentration.

Whatever it was, we'd ploughed our way awkwardly through Exodus chapter 19, which described the extraordinary phenomena of fire and thunder and shaking and sound that preceded the arrival of God at the top of Mount Sinai. My desire to find the truth that lies at the heart of every retold biblical account had led me to consider the possibility that this might be a description of an encounter with an alien spaceship, but my students decided – presumably trying to make a connection with the previous day's lesson – that it was a volcano. As if Moses would climb to the top of an erupting volcano to meet God – and survive to come back down again! Because they were so adamant that it must be a volcano (I'm sure they were now convinced that our biblical ancestors wandered around just looking for volcanoes to lead them) and because the mood seemed so strange, I decided not to waste time with other verses that I thought supported my suggestion (like Moses having radiant skin every time he encountered God and when he, his brother and nephews along with seventy elders had seen that under God's feet was '… like a pavement of sapphire, like the very sky for purity.'[12])

As no one seemed to have any enthusiasm for discussion, I decided that the best way to cope with their sluggish mood was to show them some moving pictures on a screen. I'd managed to locate Arthur C. Clarke's 2001: A Space Odyssey, and I showed the opening section, entitled 'The Dawn of Man'. It showed a deserted landscape, probably not unlike that which had confronted the wandering Israelites in the wilderness of Sinai. No matter

---

[12] Exodus 34:29 ff, 24:9-10

how often I saw it, I was always fascinated by this fictitious glimpse into the earliest days of our pre-human ancestors. My twelve-year-old audience, however, seemed unimpressed; just baffled as to why they were being made to watch these prehistoric scenes showing the struggle between two rival groups of human-like apes for possession of a pool of muddy drinking water. One group – the stronger – chases the other group away. Then one night, a mysterious monolith appears and seems to impart knowledge and inspiration to one member of the defeated group – Arthur C. Clarke names him Moonwatcher. The following day, Moonwatcher is idly playing with a bone when it suddenly dawns on him that if he uses the bone instead of his bare hands, he can wield greater power. This discovery is then eventually used to reclaim the watering-hole. The bone represents the first human use of technology. Moonwatcher hurls the bone triumphantly into the sky and the scene changes to a spaceship orbiting the earth in the year 2001.

My intention was to focus on these imagined incidents and derive from our discussions some ideas about what inspired human development and progress. So I stopped the DVD just as the bone was about to change into the spaceship, and watched, amused, as six mystified faces turned away from the screen.

'What was that all about?' asked Eric.

'A bunch of monkeys having a fight over their swimming pool?' suggested Darren.

'What's this got to do with Judaism – with religion?' added Jess's friend Julie. She looked accusingly at Jess as if to say 'why did you make me come here?' Apart from freckles and her small nose, she looked almost identical to her friend. Blue eyes, blonde hair and a mouth full of metal.

'Just stay with me guys,' I pleaded. 'Let's think about what's happening here. This is way before Judaism started. This is about how we changed from being like the other animals into a unique species. We're dealing with a time before human beings – or their predecessors – had the power of communication. This isn't history; it's pre-history. It's about how we became human.' They still looked unconvinced, so I continued.

'In that film, one group of our human ancestors is able to take control of the local water supply from another because their leader is tougher. The other group runs away. Then, one day, one member of the defeated group gets some kind of message from this weird thing that just appears overnight and suddenly realises that if he uses a bone to hit things with, it can be far more powerful than just using his bare hands.'

I looked around my group: realisation was beginning to show in their faces, just as it had on that of Moonwatcher in the film. Not surprisingly, Darren and Alison seemed to be getting there first, though it was actually Josh who spoke:

'So this thing –' he hesitated.

'Monolith,' I said, filling in the gap.

'Whatever,' he continued. 'This thing turns up from nowhere and gives the leader of this bunch of losers the idea of using a bone as a weapon ...' His voice trailed off as he still sounded uncertain, but Alison carried on.

'So something mystical planted the idea in his head, and as a result, his tribe got their water back?' It was a question, and I nodded at her, seeking to encourage.

'We don't know where inspiration comes from,' I explained. 'What we do know is that human beings – and their ancestors – have the capacity to gain sudden moments of insight that change their view of the world and their place in the world. In religious terms, we call this revelation. It always carries the sense of encountering God – whatever that means…' I paused and looked around the group, anxious to see if the mention of God broke the spell that seemed now to be holding all six of them. That was the trouble with rabbis – everything went fine until they suddenly brought God into the conversation.

'I'm not talking about some guy with a beard leaning down from a cloud and going "HEY YOU! " in a deep voice to an unsuspecting human being below,' I explained. They were shocked, then amused by my booming impersonation of the cliché of God speaking. 'That's not how revelation works, though some people would like us to believe that. Remember how Bill Cosby boomed into the microphone when God was speaking to Noah?' Three heads nodded and I remembered that the other half of the group hadn't been here for that lesson.

'So, let's look at how the bible likes us to think that revelation works,' I continued. They all reached forward with what appeared to be almost enthusiasm – Jess and Julie, who were sharing a bible, each tried to snatch their copy, with Julie emerging victorious. 'Please remember,' I added, as they opened their books, 'I'm not trying to suggest that our ancestors were the only ones who experienced revelations. It can happen to any human being at any time or place. The question is what the person – or people – experiencing it choose to do with the inspiration they receive. Our ancestors saw in it an instruction to organise their society in a particular way.' I paused, sensing that I was losing their attention. Time to get them to read.

'We already read about whatever it was that happened at Mount Sinai,' I said. 'So let's look at one that was completely different. This one happened to the prophet Elijah,' I said, as I directed my students to chapter 19 of the first book of Kings.

It was Julie who read aloud Elijah's experience of God not being in the wind or the earthquake or the fire – a description of divine revelation that seemed to be the opposite of what had happened at that same place in the book of Exodus. As Julie read the words 'soft murmuring sound,' which was the translation of the Hebrew *kol d'mammah dakkah* in the JPS[13] version we were using, I cursed myself for not having provided a different translation, one offering the 'still small voice' with which God spoke to Elijah.

I quickly jumped in with this better-known description of divine communication with Elijah. 'Which kind of encounter with God do you feel is more believable?' I asked my audience. I looked around at a collection of thoughtful faces – even Josh was sitting upright and his forehead beneath his baseball cap was wrinkled in concentration. They all agreed that hearing a still small voice alone was more credible than the supernatural phenomena

---

[13] See p.138 for author's translation.

described in Exodus 19.

I moved the conversation on, sensing that they were with me. 'Apart from the fire and thunder in Exodus, what's the other major difference between the two revelations?' There was a long silence and it was clear that this approach wasn't going to work. Now that there were six people in the group, I decided to try something else.

'Okay,' I said, 'forget that. I'd like you to work in pairs.' It was a tricky moment. I watched as each of six pairs of eyes scanned the other five members of the group and the minefield of having to pair Darren with Alison was entered. Trying to divide the group in any other way would have been completely unworkable; the question was only how Darren and Alison would react to the prospect of working together.

Ignoring the knowing looks and suppressed giggles that passed between Jess and Julie, I issued instructions that directed the two boys to look at Moses' encounter with God in Exodus chapter 3, the two girls to Jacob's revelation in Genesis 28 and the mixed group to Isaiah's vision in chapter 6 of his book. To my surprise and relief, they responded well to the task, Darren and Alison racing to find the right page without any sign of embarrassment.

The brief reporting-back exercise revealed that Jacob had encountered God in a dream after running away from the anger of his brother Esau, Moses had been spoken to from a burning bush and told that his role was to lead the Israelites out of Egypt while my friend Isaiah had seen a vision of God in the Temple in Jerusalem – a venue unknown to either Jacob or Moses.

After a few moments of discussion in pairs, Jess and Julie told the group about Jacob's encounter with God: 'He had this dream and saw angels climbing up and down a ladder to heaven,' was Jess's summary. Darren graciously deferred to Alison, allowing her to describe the *seraphim*, the strange angel-like creatures that hovered in Isaiah's vision of God in the Temple. And it was Eric who took the lead in explaining his and Josh's impressions of Moses standing before the burning bush: 'This dude saw this bush, like, on fire and when he went to look at it, it talked to him and told him to take off his shoes and it was God telling him to go rescue the Israelites from slavery – like we heard yesterday ...' Eric reported, accompanied and encouraged by vigorous nodding from Josh.

'Good job, guys,' I said. 'Let's just think a bit about these stories – what they have in common and what differences there are between each of them. Okay hands up if the person whose revelation you read about was outdoors.' Those speaking for Jacob and Moses put up their hands.

'Okay, hands up those whose encounter involved God telling them to do something.' Alison looked towards Darren before they raised their hands on Isaiah's behalf, accompanied by Eric and Josh both saying 'Yo!'

'And hands up those whose person saw a vision rather than something real.' Jess and Julie raised their hands immediately. Darren and Alison checked with each other once again before doing likewise.

Josh pushed himself up from his prone position to rest on his elbows and protested: 'What's to say that the burning bush Moses saw was real? He might have been seeing things.'

'They all might!' shouted Eric, laughing. 'Maybe they were all nuts!'

Everyone laughed – Josh lay back on the ground and waved his arms and legs in the air.

'Okay so what do you guys think Moses saw?' I said, throwing it back at them.

'A talking burning bush,' said Eric, rolling his eyes as he spoke. I wasn't sure whether he was ridiculing the idea of such a thing or me for asking a question that he had already answered.

'And do you think that's likely?' I asked, my tone trying to encourage them to say no.

'Well, not really,' said Alison, tentatively. Darren, sitting alongside her, nodded slowly.

'Is it another one of those stories that grew each time it was told?' he asked.

'Maybe,' I agreed. 'But there's another important point here. What have all three of these revelations got in common?' I didn't let the silence go on for too long – I wanted to keep the momentum going. 'Who else was there when Isaiah, Moses and Jacob encountered God?' I asked, quickly adding 'Apart from God …' before any of them tried that one.

'They were all on their own,' said Alison at the same time as Julie said 'No one.'

'Exactly,' I went on. 'And if there was no one else there apart from them, how can we be sure what they actually saw or experienced. And that's true of all revelations in the bible, except for the one we read at the beginning, the one at Sinai.' I paused for a moment and watched realisation dawn slowly on their faces.

'So if no one else was there, who knows what they saw anyway?' demanded Josh indignantly.

'Exactly,' I confirmed, acknowledging Josh's observation. 'Moses makes the point in his conversation with the burning bush – can someone read Exodus chapter 3 verse 13?'

Eric was the first to grab his copy of the *Tanakh* and read: 'Moses said to God, "When I come to the Israelites and say to them, 'The God of your fathers has sent me to you,' and they ask me, "What is his name?" What shall I say to them?"' Eric looked up.

'So even Moses doesn't believe what he's just seen or heard,' I continued. 'And his first worry is how he's going to convince everyone else. But what do you think he actually saw?' There was another uncertain pause so I moved on quickly. 'Take a look at this,' I said, handing round my mobile phone. The screensaver showed a picture of an extraordinary sunset through some trees that I had taken from the passenger seat of a car while driving near my home in Hertfordshire.[14]

---

[14] This image is the background of the front cover of this book.

Responses varied: Jess and Julie both said 'Cool!' and giggled, Josh and Eric looked at it in turn and said nothing before passing it to Alison who nodded, then Darren who said 'a burning bush!'

'And that's a burning bush that I saw near my home in England, not in the middle of a wilderness!' I exclaimed. 'And maybe that's all Moses saw – a sunset that looked like a burning bush. And maybe the voice of God spoke within him, making him realise that he should go back to Egypt and save his people. And that's what matters: it's not what he saw or heard, but what he did as a result of that experience.' I looked around the group again and saw that, with the possible exception of Josh, who had resumed his position lying on his back staring upwards at the sky, there seemed to be understanding.

'And the point of these revelations is that it really doesn't matter what was seen, or how the person – or people – concerned experienced God. It's fun to speculate about what it might have been but what's really important is what happens as a result of that encounter. The important thing about Moses' revelation at the burning bush was that as a result of it, he found the courage to go back to Egypt and lead his people to freedom.' I had the sense that my enthusiasm was rubbing off on my young audience. Even Josh's head was tilted towards me, I noted, as I scanned the group. 'The important thing about whatever happened at Mount Sinai – spaceship, volcano or whatever it might have been – was that the Israelite people developed their idea of one God and of that one God being the source of laws – we'll get back to that soon.'

Our lesson was reaching its conclusion, as was the after lunch break. There were several people making their way to various locations on camp, indicating that afternoon sessions were about to start. But I had one more thing to say. 'And the important thing about the Exodus that we talked about yesterday was not whether it was a volcano or an angry God having a playground fight with an Egyptian leader, though again, it's fun to try and work out what really happened. What really matters is that at the start of the story a group of people were slaves and by the end of it, they were free. And that experience taught them the importance of freedom.'

I looked around at six faces, each of which appeared to show some understanding. As they each rose, offering their farewells to me and one another, a recognition of the opportunity I had to bring such moments of insight to young minds passed through me. Like old Moonwatcher in that barren, prehistoric wilderness, I felt I wanted to throw something into the air with joy.

* * * * * * * * * * * *

The seventh encounter – Thursday night

'I decided not to make too much of your revelation – the vision in the Temple,' I said, a little hesitantly. I felt a bit embarrassed but this was something I really wanted to talk about. He said nothing. 'I was trying to keep it uncomplicated, talking to the kids about encountering God in simple ways and, er, to be honest, I thought yours was a bit, well, unbelievable really ...'

My words hung in the air and I braced myself for his reaction. But it was true. Talking to twelve-year-olds – or anyone really – about encounters with God was always a bit tricky. People would smile indulgently or look at the floor, waiting patiently for you to finish whatever you might be saying about your personal experiences of the divine and then quickly change the subject.

So I'd chosen the biblical episodes of revelation carefully to try and demonstrate that, apart from whatever it was that happened at Mount Sinai, encounters with God were to be found in everyday experiences, dreams or moments of silence. So that's why I'd gone into detail about the stories of Moses, Jacob and Elijah rather than that of Isaiah, whose encounter in the Temple was too loaded with mythical figures and improbable experiences to fit very comfortably with a modern audience.

'Surely you do not think it was supposed to be true?' he asked. 'It was our tradition – to present to our listeners tales of elaborate experiences of the Eternal One to add weight to the instructions and criticisms we were imparting to them. I suppose you might call it dramatic effect,' he concluded.

'So that account of the seraphim and the Temple shaking and the hot coal on your lips was all just made up?' I asked, feeling bewildered.

'Of course,' he said indignantly. 'The people who heard us describing those visions knew that it was just a part of our performance, designed to capture their attention and give more credibility to the demands that we intended to make of them. I am dismayed that in this age that claims to know so much more than mine, such devices are regarded as being literal truth.' I could sense him shaking his head. 'It is no different from your sitting here having a conversation with a tree that purports to speak with the voice of a biblical prophet. What you are doing is reflecting on the origins and purpose of this book you call the Torah and our conversations are a manifestation of your endeavour to understand this. Encounters with God operate in a similar manner.'

'So how do we encounter God?' I asked quietly.

'Naturally,' he replied. 'Remember the story you told about that northern prophet, Elijah. It was brilliantly written by a northern author, deliberately constructed to explain that an encounter with God does not require grand displays and dramatic effects. God's presence, inspiring within us an understanding of our human responsibility to establish justice, is to be found whenever and wherever we open ourselves to its possibility. We do not need special times or places or words or people, though these can sometimes help us to focus on what is required of us. The danger is when we allow those times and places to distract us from the true purpose of religion.'

'Which is?' I asked, though I was sure I already knew the answer.

'To focus our minds on the basic truth that our human duty is to bring justice and harmony to this world. And then to go out into that world and make that a reality. God is a name for that invisible presence at the heart of creation that seeks to make us aware of that duty and responsibility. Worship is to remind us of that; it is not meant to be the elaborate performance that it has become.'

'That's just bullocks,' I said.

'Take care,' he warned, 'for there is value in ritual and tradition – in bullocks as you define it – and to dismiss it completely diminishes our connection with the Eternal One. Human beings can be extremely shallow. I witnessed it in my time and I see it here also. The function of worship is to remind us that there is depth and significance to our lives, that there is a greater purpose for which we have been created. In my day it was fear that brought people to places of worship, a sense of weakness in the face of an extraordinary power that held their lives in its grasp. Incidents of drought, famine or other natural catastrophe were seen as manifestations of a force that controlled people's lives. Events like the earthquake that devastated the lands of Judah and Israel in my time or the volcano that affected Egypt of which you spoke the other day were seen as punishment from an angry God. And so ritual correctness was seen as a means of influencing that force, of encouraging it to show kindness to the people. Much of it was little more than superstition. We – the prophets as you call us – made use of that awesome respect that sometimes bordered on fear, to heighten the people's awareness of their duty to establish justice. Without very much success,' he added as an afterthought.

'But your world has greater knowledge of how this force operates. You do not respect it, you exploit it. You do not fear it, you challenge it. Only when it threatens or hurts you do you pay it any attention. Mostly you simply take it for granted. And so you do not see a need for ritual. Unlike the people in my time, you know that words and songs and certain prescribed behaviour will not influence the forces that sustain the universe.'

'But their purpose is to influence you; to increase your awareness of your place within that universe and your responsibility to its development. Human beings are no longer frightened little children who dutifully seek to please or pacify their parent. Perhaps you have become adolescents, stubborn and rebellious children who think only of yourselves. Ritual is important to remind you of your obligations and of your potential; you should not dismiss it lightly.'

I felt as though I were being chastised. I waited for his final words of judgement. When they came, they were less harsh than I had feared.

'But what you seek to teach your young charges is mainly correct,' he continued. 'To follow ritual and tradition without question is not correct. What I have heard about the literal reading and application of my words and the words of others is an insult to humanity – and to us. How can anyone fail to see that what we wrote was intended for our time and that each generation must seek its own solutions? But that search must be conducted with respect for creation and an understanding of the human potential that needs and yearns to be fulfilled.'

'And ritual can encourage that?' I asked tentatively.

'If conducted in the proper spirit, yes,' he replied. 'A spirit of humility and respect, a searching, a quest for understanding and growth. Where ritual and prayer are part of the journey, not the destination. And you have the good fortune to be guiding young students towards that destination at a key stage on their journey. Your role is to teach them to learn from the past, to use the ritual and the tradition to make sense of the present and seek to shape the future, to play their part in moving this ancient tradition and this troubled human race forwards from where it is to where it can be. And to achieve this, they need to seek out that in our ancient faith which contains truth and wisdom, to separate that which has meaning –'

'– from the bullocks,' I concluded.

He laughed indulgently. 'A useful, if rather crude and overused distinction,' he said. A silence followed.

'So how can we rediscover that respect?' I asked eventually.

'By studying the way that we understood the world in my time,' was his reply. 'Look at the ways in which we regarded nature's manifestations, how we struggled to make sense of happenings that to you are now easily explained and too readily ignored. You may laugh at some of our practices and choose – quite rightly – to dismiss them as products of their time. But remember that they are products of a time that truly appreciated how precarious life is and that managed to sense God's influence in even the most everyday things. Your progress in knowledge and understanding is at the expense of awareness and respect. And observing the religious heritage that has been passed down to you should be a joyous celebration, not a tired duty.

'We understood how fortunate we were to be blessed with God's gifts! And we gave our thanks with heartfelt joy and gratitude! We knew terror and awe but we also knew joy and celebration. Our festivals were truly wonderful occasions where we acknowledged and thanked the Eternal One for the beautiful things that we had been granted. But you have taken our terror and our awe and our joy and our celebration and made them serious, self-indulgent and dull. And you have filled your world with explanation, leaving no room for appreciation. You live in a world that does not see or hear God.'

I was nodding as he spoke. 'I can't argue with that,' I said. 'But how can we reintroduce God to a world that fails to acknowledge the presence of the divine, that refuses to recognise God in everyday life? Even saying that feels faintly ridiculous to me – so it's no wonder that Josh and company would just laugh and mock the whole notion.'

'It is not too difficult for you or too remote,' he said. 'It is not in the heavens that you might say, "who will go up to the heavens for us to fetch it and explain it to us that we might do it?" And it is not beyond the sea that you might say "who will go across the sea for us to fetch it and explain it to us that we might do it? " No, this thing is very near to you: on your lips and in your heart that you might do it.

'That is how you find God and fulfil your human potential,' he concluded.

'Did you write that?' I asked, astonished and delighted to have heard my favourite words from the book of Deuteronomy[15].

'I might,' he replied enigmatically.

* * * * * * * * * * * *

As usual, my late-night encounter in the rarefied air of this Californian Jewish summer camp left me feeling uplifted and inspired. I felt as though I suddenly recognised that the

---

[15] Deuteronomy 30:11-13

purpose of the ancient rituals that had become – and still were – a part of Judaism was to foster a sense of respect and awe. I paused on my walk back to my cabin to gaze once again at the bright night sky above me and tried to register some of that awe at the magnitude and beauty not just of the sight my eyes beheld but also at the intricacies of the various physical forces and phenomena that combined to permit life on this tiny planet.

There had to be some way to impart this sense of appreciation to my twenty-first century Californian twelve-year-olds surrounded by their cocooned air-conditioned lifestyles and labour saving devices. I stared for a while at a blank computer screen, searching for inspiration for ways to present to my students the magnificence of nature and their ancestors' respect for it, but eventually concluded that there was really only one way: tell them about it. In order to assist with this, I would have to take some time to prepare some very basic diagrams about the earth's rotation around the sun and the phases of the moon. I had no idea that nature herself was actually planning to lend me a hand …

LESSON SEVEN – Friday afternoon

'Experiencing God'

The seven of us reached the sanctuary of the study room more or less simultaneously. I was pleased that I had not been the last to arrive, having succeeded in keeping pace with these youngsters as we all raced to escape from the torrential rain. Rain in California! Apparently this was something truly rare and the reaction of the Californians to it was equally precious.

For an Englishman, the sight of rain in July was commonplace but here on the sun-drenched west coast of the United States of America, it was a different story. I watched with amusement as my six twelve-year-olds fought for breath, excitement in their eyes as they looked at each other and then through the open door at the torrents of falling rain that sheeted down outside. Beyond those doors, several of their fellow campers could be seen dancing in the rain, enjoying the opportunity of an outdoor shower – fully-clothed of course – in the early afternoon. Darren shook his head like a drenched poodle and managed to splash all three of the girls nearby. Eric used the tips of his fingers to wipe the water from his eyes and cheekbones while Josh inspected his baseball cap with concern, as though fearing that it might shrivel before his eyes.

It had been raining for almost half an hour now. It had begun during lunch, and the sound of the rain falling on the metal roof of the dining hall had been extraordinary, as had the reaction of the people inside. After the initial shock of the noise, there had been excitement and laughter and the campers' journeys back to their cabins had been filled with screams – of joy, discomfort, fear or exhilaration.

I had avoided the directors' crisis meeting to discuss the rescheduling of the afternoon's programme to set up my *bar-/bat-mitzvah* session indoors. And here it was, ready for my students who had dutifully turned up at the tree as requested (I had located them all during lunch and told them we would meet under it as normal) and then sprinted with me for cover in this large hall. It was a multi-purpose hall that could comfortably hold well over two hundred people, so the seven of us took up only a fraction of its space. In one corner, I had placed six chairs in a small semi-circle, facing a flipchart and I directed my damp charges in that direction once the novelty (though not the reality) of being wet had worn off.

There were various groans of discomfort (most of them from Julie and Jess) as their wet clothes pressed against them as they sat down. I couldn't help laughing at them – particularly the two complaining girls whose normally groomed hair looked particularly bedraggled and whose smudged faces revealed that they did not entirely adhere to the camp's policy of no make-up.

'It seems to be raining,' I said with a smile, once they had finally settled. They laughed uncertainly – they couldn't quite get the hang of British understatement. 'Which is quite funny really, because that's the focus of what I want to talk about today,' I continued.

'Thousands of years ago, early human beings had very little understanding of how the world worked,' I began. 'Think of those ape-like creatures we were watching yesterday. They had no idea where rain came from, or why some days were cold and others were hot. They didn't know what made them get sick – and why some of them died while others recovered. That's why the discovery of the use of that bone as a weapon was so crucial – it was a huge step on our ancestors' journey to understand and take control of their world. But it was – and still is – a long journey.'

I paused and looked around. The six of them seemed to have forgotten their damp discomfort and were all listening closely. 'And slowly, they began to notice things about their world, patterns in the way things happened. Like how at certain times it would be really hot while others would be colder.'

'Seasons!' interrupted Darren.

'Exactly, I said, and turned over the first sheet on the flip-chart on which I had earlier drawn a rather crude diagram of the earth's rotation around the sun. 'And here's why we have seasons,' I continued, quickly explaining how the tilt of the earth meant that at certain points during the solar year the northern hemisphere was closer to the sun and further away at other times. The responses to my questions about the names of the seasons came from Alison and Eric. I saw Josh's face wrinkle with mounting disapproval and awaited the inevitable protest.

'What's this got to do with religion?' he sneered.

'Everything,' I replied. 'Because religion is all about how to deal with what life throws at us. Remember, I'm talking about how the earliest humans learned to cope with their world, long before Israelites or Jews were on the scene. We're talking about how people slowly began to understand that there were certain physical laws that gave order to their existence. And if you don't understand that the earth moves around the sun and that everything goes in cycles, you've got no idea what's going to happen next.' Six blank expressions. Time to change tack and get them to think about those cycles, the patterns of nature that governed their lives without them even realising it.

'We're in the middle of summer, right?' I asked, evoking a response of five nodding heads. Josh was motionless, uncertain – presumably of where this was going, not of the fact that it was summer. 'So when will it get dark tonight – when will Shabbat officially start?' I added, suddenly remembering that it was Friday and that sunset was when the Sabbath was deemed to start, although the camp would welcome it several hours before that time.

'About 9.30,' said Darren.

'And if it was December, when would it get dark?' I asked.

'Way earlier than that,' answered Alison.

'Right,' I said, moving to the flipchart and putting a very child-like drawing of a house at the bottom right hand corner of the sheet. 'Okay this is the camp,' I said, to a chorus of laughs. 'If we could see the sun now, in the middle of the day, where would it be in the sky?' They agreed that it would be directly above us, so I drew it high above the little house. 'And if it was a sunny day in winter?'

'Much lower,' said Darren.

I quickly explained about the position of the sun on the horizon during the year, the winter and summer solstices and the spring and autumn equinoxes, rapidly changing 'autumn' to 'fall' in response to their blank expressions. Josh still looked suspicious.

'Stay with me, Josh,' I said. 'In the depths of winter, early humans were frightened that the sun, getting lower in the sky every day, might just disappear for ever. And in the summer, as it got hotter and hotter, they were scared the sun would shine longer and longer. But gradually they recognised there was a pattern, that the sun reached a low point then started getting higher again – and the opposite in the summer.' All the time I was talking I was scribbling on my little picture, covering the sky above the little house with suns in various positions.

'Here's the point where the sun is at its highest,' I said, moving to my diagram of the earth's rotation to indicate the point where the little 'x' that marked ancient Israel was closest to the sun. 'And what do we call this?' 'Summer.' I wasn't sure who had said this – there were at least two voices, possibly three. 'And this one?' I asked, pointing to the opposite side of the sheet. All bar Josh joined in the chorus saying 'winter.'

'And as our ancestors began to recognise the repeating cycle of the seasons, they also noticed how the earth and life on it responded to those seasons. What happens in the spring?' I sat myself down in a nearby chair, indicating that it was time for them to do the talking.

'The weather gets better?' suggested Alison. I nodded, and beckoned with my hands, trying to draw more information from them.

'Stuff starts to grow?' said Julie, uncertainly.

'That's right!' I exclaimed. 'And what's a symbol of that?' I looked directly at Julie, willing her to continue, but she just shook her head at me. Jess cried 'Yeuggh!' as the water that had splashed from Julie's hair hit her cheek. Both girls laughed.

'Come on!' I urged. 'What animal is born in spring and is seen as a symbol of that time of year?'

It was Darren who was the first to say 'Lambs.'

'Great stuff,' I said, conscious that I sounded very English. 'And what about the autumn – sorry – fall?' We all agreed – with the exception of Josh who was still sulkily silent – that this was a time when summer ended and the weather started to get worse as the climate headed into winter once more. 'Okay,' I said, jumping from my chair and pointing to the two opposite points of the solar year on my diagram, 'which of these do you think was more significant for our ancient ancestors?'

'Spring,' declared Darren confidently.

'Why?' I challenged.

'Because it's the end of winter, showing that the people have survived the cold and there's the promise of the summer ahead,' he replied.

'Okay,' I agreed, nodding. 'But in a society that's based on agriculture, that depends for its survival on food growing from the earth, there's something really crucial that happens at the end of the summer …' I let my voice fade, waiting for someone to conclude my train of thought.

'The harvest?' asked Alison, tilting her head to one side as she spoke.

'You got it!' I exclaimed. 'The harvest in the autumn –' I tutted and rolled my eyes at them '– fall – was the crucial time of the year. First of all, the people had to gather in all their food and store it so that they had enough to get them through the winter until stuff started growing again in the spring. It was a time of great joy as they ate and drank and celebrated all the wonderful things that had come from the earth.' I tried to sound as though I was as joyful as my ancient Israelite ancestors at the harvest time, though I doubted that I could really empathise with what their feelings would have been as they celebrated the gathering of the earth's bounty. 'And they believed that these things had been given to them by some power that watched over them, so they gave thanks to that power with songs and sacrifices – we talked about that already.' A pause. 'But there was anxiety as well.' I changed the tone of my voice, trying to make it sound anxious.

'Why were they worried?' asked Jess

'Okay. Simple questions,' I said, wanting to move this along. 'What was the weather like through the summer and while they gathered their harvest? Darren?' I fired the question quickly, and he responded in similar fashion.

'Hot and dry.'

'Good. And what was the ground like? Alison?'

She paused momentarily, then said, 'Dry and hard.'

'Yep,' I replied. 'Okay Julie – what would you need to do once you've taken the food out of the ground?'

Julie screwed up her face into a confused expression. 'Anyone?'

'Plant seeds for the next year?' ventured Eric.

'Exactly Eric,' I said, taking a sudden step towards them. 'But at the end of the summer, you have a problem, which is …?' I held out my hands, pleading silently with them to answer the question that I considered to be blindingly obvious.

'The ground's too hard,' growled Josh, without moving his eyes from the window.

'So what do you need?' I asked, aiming my question at all of them but knowing who was going to answer it.

Josh turned to face me triumphantly. 'Rain,' he said simply, pointing at the window with a wry smile. As if on cue, the other five turned to look out of the window. The rain was still falling as heavily as ever, bouncing off the concrete roadway outside the building.

I nodded my approval at Josh. 'Exactly,' I confirmed, speaking in a quiet voice. 'Remember, our ancestors had no real idea where rain came from – they didn't understand anything about how the world worked. All they knew was that at the end of the long summer, once they'd gathered in their harvest, they needed a bit of rain to soften the ground, just enough for them to be able to plant their seeds – not too much or they'd all get washed away. Then a dry period to let them do the planting, then heavier rain to water their seeds and let them grow. And – guess what?' I extended my arms like a magician about to conclude a trick. 'That's exactly what happened!'

A short interlude followed while we looked in the bible at a section of the book of Deuteronomy that was part of the traditional version of the *Sh'ma* – the second paragraph, not a part of Liberal liturgy[16]. It talked of God's promise to send the early and the late rain – exactly the rain that our ancestors needed just after the harvest time.

'So they believed that God sent the rain – exactly at the time and in the amount that they wanted,' I continued. 'Now, do you remember the account of the second day of creation in the first chapter of Genesis? It talks about the sky separating the waters above from the waters below. So that was their idea of where rain –' I gestured towards the window '– comes from.'

I moved things along quickly, confirming that they'd got the idea that rain falling after the harvest was crucial for the people's survival. 'So they got everyone together once the harvest was over and got them to thank God for all the food. And, like I already said, they just had a great celebration – they were delighted at how wonderful the world was. But as well as celebrating, they were also asking for rain.' I paused and looked at each of them in turn. 'What's the main symbol of the harvest festival we still celebrate today?'

'The *sukkah*?' That was Jess.

---

[16] Deuteronomy 11:13-21

'You're right, Jess,' I said, and quickly explained the origin and practical purpose of this temporary hut, made of branches and built in the middle of the field to allow the farmers to keep watch over the crops they had gathered in and to save them commuting to and from the fields every day at harvest time.

'But there's something else,' I continued. 'What do we wave at the harvest festival?' It wasn't long before they came up with the answer of the *lulav*, the palm branch. 'And what do you think that's supposed to do?' I asked, mimicking the strange *Sukkot* ritual, with the sharp tip of the palm branch pointed at the sky.

'Poke holes in the sky!' exclaimed Julie, and the others laughed.

'You're right,' I confirmed, explaining that this ancient ritual seemed to be an attempt to pierce holes in the sky, in order to encourage or facilitate the release of the 'waters above'. 'Not only that,' I added, 'but shaking a *lulav* – or lots of people shaking them together – actually sounds like falling rain.' My listeners looked doubtful. 'It's true!' I exclaimed. 'And that took place during the ancient festival of *Sukkot*. Who can tell me when that happens?'

'In the fall,' ventured Josh. 'Yes Josh,' I replied, trying to sound encouraging. 'But do you know the actual date? Or the month maybe?'

'The month of *Tishri*,' said Alison.

I nodded. 'That's right. Anyone know what date?'

They clearly weren't going to get this, so it was up to me to point out to them that it was the fifteenth day of that month. I then flipped to the next sheet on which I had prepared a diagram of the phases of the moon. I quickly explained how the ancients had measured time using those lunar phases and that *Sukkot*, the harvest festival, was celebrated when the moon was full, on the fifteenth day of the month. Then I switched back to the previous sheet with the diagram of the earth's rotation, and pointed to the position at the autumn equinox.

'So at this time of the year when the moon was full, our ancestors celebrated an eight day long harvest festival. The bible actually described it as a seven-day festival with an eighth day of conclusion.[17] Full moon, seventh month of the year.'

'How come it's the seventh month?' asked Darren.

'Thank you for asking that,' I said, smiling. 'Because our ancestors counted the start of the year from the spring, the time when the earth first showed signs of coming back to life.' I pointed to the earth in its spring equinox position. 'Right here. Exactly the opposite point from the harvest. And they celebrated a special festival there as well. What's the Jewish

---

[17] Leviticus 23:36

spring festival called?'

'Pesach!' Two voices – Jess and Darren, I thought, though I couldn't be sure. But I did notice that Josh seemed to be fully engaged again.

'And anyone know the Hebrew date of that one?' They didn't, so I told them. 'The fifteenth day of Nisan – the first month.' I indicated the relative positions of these two major festivals on my diagram: 'The seven day festival of *Sukkot*, the autumn – sorry, fall – harvest is celebrated when the moon is full after the harvest has been gathered and the seven day festival of Pesach happens on the full moon once the winter is past. And the concluding day of *Sukkot* is a day later, while in the spring they had to wait another seven weeks before celebrating the harvest of the first fruits – *Shavu'ot*. At this point, I was assuming that they had a basic Jewish religious knowledge – there wasn't really time to explain the seven weeks between *Pesach* and *Shavu'ot*. No one protested, so I assumed they got it. 'Ancient, ancient festivals that pre-date Judaism or ancient Israelite religion by hundreds and hundreds of years. They emphasise humanity's dependence on nature, their gratitude for what it gave them and their fear that it might let them down. These two ancient celebrations at these crucial turning points in the year were adopted by the Israelites, and became the backbone of our ancestors' faith, linked entirely to the seasons.'

I stepped back from the flipchart, and surveyed my audience. They seemed to be reasonably attentive, though it was unusual to see them in chairs rather than in various positions stretched out on the grass beneath the tree. They seemed to be thinking – I hoped they were taking in the ancient agricultural roots of their religious heritage.

'So how come we have to eat matzah at Pesach?' It was Josh, who seemed to have decided to stop looking through the window now that the rain had ceased.

'Because it was a time for spring cleaning,' I replied. 'The people had lived cooped up in their houses all through the winter, using their supply of fermented dough to make bread. The change of weather offered by the spring was a chance to clean everything out and start again. So they had a seven-day period eating bread without any yeast in it at all after which they started using new yeast for the coming year.' They looked at me blankly, so I just said 'Basically, it was getting rid of the stuff they'd been using to make bread for the last year as it could have been going rotten and allowing seven days for a new batch to become ready – and so they ate unleavened bread in the meantime.'

'So what's the story about them having to make the bread in a hurry as they left Egypt so there wasn't time for it to rise?' challenged Josh.

'That's what I'd call bullocks,' I said, with a smile. They looked confused. 'It's just an explanation or interpretation that was added later to give a modern reason for an ancient practice. People were eating unleavened bread in the spring for hundreds of years before the Exodus from Egypt took place. But it was a time of liberation – from the winter – so it seemed a good time to recall the Exodus story as well.

'And talking of the Exodus,' I concluded, 'It's time you guys were on your way out of here. The rain has stopped and it looks as though everything is returning to normal.' The brief empathy with their biblical ancestors at the sight of rain had passed and they returned to the familiarity of their regular Californian climate. I wondered if the experience had given them any insight into their ancestors' dependence on and appreciation of nature as I turned to fold up my diagrams of the earth's movement around the sun.

The eighth encounter – Friday night

'Shabbat Shalom!' There was genuine warmth in his greeting as I arrived for our nightly encounter. 'A simple phrase that I have heard so many times this evening,' he continued, 'bringing with it so much warmth and hope.' The spirit of the Sabbath seemed to have settled over the entire camp, an indefinable sense of peace and calm following the special weekly celebrations to welcome this ancient day of rest. The camp tradition was for everyone to dress in white and for the whole camp to come together for a service to welcome Shabbat, followed by a celebratory meal.

'This idea of welcoming the Sabbath is an extraordinary concept,' he said. 'I am filled with admiration for the sense of community it engenders, the spirit of joy that it fosters. That is exactly the type of celebration I was talking about last night. You must tell me more about its origins, its traditions and its significance.'

And so I found myself in the peculiar position of explaining to an eighth century BCE Israelite prophet the history and development of the Jewish Sabbath. He already knew how the Israelite lawmakers recognised the importance of allowing every living creature the opportunity to rest every seventh day, but what was new to him were the customs used to celebrate that day. As I was telling him, it occurred to me that most of the traditions I was describing – lighting candles, singing and praying, holding special religious services – had been introduced by rabbis who lived several centuries after Isaiah.

'What you just saw was a very liberal interpretation of Shabbat,' I continued, pointing out that the playing of guitars, the use of electricity or motor vehicles, such as the ones I could see at the bottom of the hill returning some staff members to the car park, would not be tolerated in an Orthodox Jewish environment.

'I believe the time has arrived for you to explain to me the distinction between Orthodox and Liberal Judaism that you have promised,' he said. I agreed, realising that the observance of the Sabbath was actually the ideal area to describe the distinctions between these two versions of his and my faith.

And so I began by reminding him about the Torah, the document that according to Orthodox tradition had been received by Moses at Mount Sinai some five centuries before he had lived and of whose existence – and purported author – he had no knowledge.

'The ancient Rabbis, who lived several centuries after your time, were the ones who initiated the idea that this document had been written by God,' I continued. 'As such, it became necessary to create regulations to ensure that no law contained within it was breached. And so these teachers of Judaism created a system of regulations designed to 'put a fence around the Torah' as they described it. So, for example, when the Torah said that no work should be done on the Sabbath, they first of all defined what work was and then proceeded to establish regulations to prevent anyone from doing anything that might even come close to being seen as work, and thus a breach of a divine law.

'Let's use the playing of guitars as an example,' I went on, getting into full flow now. 'Nowhere in the Torah does it say that a guitar should not be played on Shabbat – indeed as you know, musical instruments were a feature of worship in your day.'

'Before the Torah was written ...' he reminded me.

I nodded. 'But if a guitar is played, it's possible that a string might break. If a string breaks, the player might be tempted to repair it and, in so doing, he would be engaging in work and thereby breaching a fundamental law of the Sabbath.'

'But guitars were played at the service and at the celebration of song that took place afterwards,' he said.

'Which is a perfect example of the difference between Liberal and Orthodox Judaism,' I responded. 'Liberal Judaism believes that the spirit of a law is more important than rigid adherence to its letter. We believe, as Jews have ever since they began worshipping, that music enhances the experience of worship and enables us, as you have already said, to celebrate more joyfully. To prohibit the playing of musical instruments that will elevate the experience of Shabbat on the basis of a two thousand-year-old rabbinic interpretation of biblical verses believed to be a thousand years older than that seems to us Liberal Jews to be, well, silly to say the least.'

'Those biblical verses were not written a thousand years before the rabbis,' he chided me. 'They did not even exist in any formal way in my time, remember?'

'I know that,' I confirmed. 'And that, in the end, is the major difference between Liberal and Orthodox Judaism. Liberal Jews firmly believe that this document at the heart of our tradition is a human document, the record of our ancestors' attempt to make sense of their world and to find meaning and purpose within that world. Orthodox Jews believe that God wrote the entire Torah, or dictated it to Moses at Mount Sinai, exactly as described in the Torah itself.'

'So how does this Orthodox belief manifest itself – apart from prohibiting the playing of guitars on Shabbat?' he asked.

I provided some more examples, continuing to use the observance of Shabbat as a way of differentiating between Orthodox and Liberal Judaism. I described the *eruv*, the imaginary boundary that on Shabbat turned everything within it into a public area, allowing Orthodox Jews to get around the law in the book of Exodus commanding that no one should leave his own place on the Sabbath and permit them to carry personal items or push prams, for example. I talked about the Orthodox prohibition against travelling, which often led to those people visiting Orthodox synagogues driving most of the way to the synagogue and then walking the final stretch, as though trying to convince their fellow congregants that they had walked the entire distance. He laughed when I explained to him that a former British Chief Rabbi had once justified this Orthodox approach to Judaism as being more worthy than its Liberal counterpart because at least the Orthodox Jew acknowledged what it was he should be doing even if he didn't actually do it.

'This all sounds suspiciously like bullocks to me,' was his comment. 'Now tell me how Liberal Judaism is different.'

'Liberal Judaism was born at the beginning of the nineteenth century, a time of enormous change,' I began. 'One of those changes was that people began to recognise discrepancies in the biblical texts that suggested they could not have been written by a single source. This led to a shift away from a form of Judaism that had been practised almost unchanged for centuries in the enclosed communities where Jews lived in isolation from the world around them. For those Jews taking the modern view, the observance of their ancient religion could no longer be regarded as carrying out the will of God. The existence of other religions made it obvious that God's will manifested itself in various ways and, as I mentioned, it was also becoming clear that whoever had written the Torah, it wasn't God.

'And so Liberal Judaism developed the understanding that God had inspired the authors of the Torah to try to introduce a religious awareness and a code of laws that would lead to the establishment of a society in which there was justice for all. The important thing was not the laws themselves, rather the desire for justice that led to their introduction. And so Liberal Judaism sought to rediscover that desire, embodied in the visions of the prophets, and refocus Judaism on that goal. We still keep some of the rituals – like lighting candles to welcome Shabbat on Friday night and gathering together as a community to pray together, as you just saw – but ultimately these are meant to remind and encourage us to engage in the work of establishing justice.'

'You are right to say that the purpose of community prayer is to encourage the search for justice,' was his response. 'That is a subject to which we shall return. But there is a deeper purpose to religious ritual, an attempt to commune with forces outside and beyond our everyday experience. The Sabbath is about establishing and acknowledging a part of time that is devoted to a higher purpose,' he said, rather cryptically. 'There are boundaries to everyday human experience and there are boundaries to the realm in which God exists.'

I was puzzled.

'The setting aside of time to approach that boundary is a critical element of the religious experience,' he continued. 'And so is the setting aside of particular places – and even people to manage those places.' I really wasn't sure where this was going. 'Rituals exist to help us to approach that which is other. There is a mystery at the core of the plainest things and we approach that mystery in ways that emphasise the distinction between the human and the divine.'

I was getting lost and it was time to tell him so. 'What are you talking about?'

He laughed. 'I am talking about the need for *k'dushah,* which you translate as holiness. It is a bad translation, for what it really means is the setting aside of time, of space, and carrying out particular activities in those special times and places. In other words, you need the rituals and symbols of religion to remind you that you are engaged in an activity that is approaching the boundary between the human and the divine. You are right to seek to rationalise religious practice in the Liberal manner that you describe. But you cannot dispense with the mystery or you fall victim to the same trap that has ensnared the scientists of your age.

'Of course, religion has also fallen into many traps,' he continued. 'The belief in the absolute correctness of one particular approach to the mystery and the consequent falsity of any alternative approach. The over-elaboration of ritual that serves only to distract from the true object of the exercise.'

'Which is?'

'What we have already discussed: to find value and meaning in life and to continue human progress towards what humanity can and must become. And that will be achieved neither by dogmatic adherence to outdated ritual and practice nor by the rejection of the mystery that first inspired such ritual and practice.'

I still wasn't sure where he was going with this but I guessed that all would soon become clear. It did.

'Throughout the ages, human beings have turned towards that mystery and sought to communicate with it in different ways. To ignore this connection, this need, is to ignore an essential element of our humanity. It is at the heart of religion, the core of the quest for understanding. If an awareness of that mystery is not at the heart of the religious quest, then it ceases to be a religious quest and becomes merely scientific exploration, interested only in explanation but not in meaning.

'Your task is to search for meaning. Explore that which underlies your religious traditions – even those you have rejected, because they were also the result of searching – and you will truly be engaged in that same search.'

My journey back to my cabin was a thoughtful one as I struggled to comprehend the words of the prophet and then to turn those words into something that I could teach to my group of twelve-year-olds.

* * * * * * * * * * * *

By the time I was seated in front of my computer, the struggle was beginning to ease. We had looked at the mythical stories in the Torah that had given the earliest Israelites a sense of their origins. We had moved from there to an awareness of how the earliest humans had begun to understand the workings of nature and recognise in them the presence and influence of a divine power. Now it was time to move the project forward and look at how our biblical ancestors approached and treated that mystery. Sacrifices and priests, mystery and awe – these were the features of the biblical relationship with the divine. The question was how to present this to my students in a way that would give them a sense of the mystery and the awe that filled the lives of their ancient ancestors.

I recalled a scene from the film 'Raiders of the Lost Ark'. The final scene, where fire came from the ark and consumed all those present, would be a useful way of introducing the terror that 'crossing the boundary' between the human and the divine could induce. And, as I recalled, there was a good explanation of the history and role of the Ark, provided by Indiana Jones himself. I was sure I could dig out those scenes and use them to help me explain how the ancients believed it was necessary to have special people to approach God on their behalf in order to protect them from manifestations of divine power.

LESSON EIGHT – Saturday afternoon

'Talking to God'

It was a lazy Californian Shabbat afternoon. Compared to the panic-stricken reaction to the rain of twenty-four hours earlier, the camp was a model of calm, preparing for a series of gentle activities designed to promote a sense of Sabbath peace. Nature was once again behaving as Californians believed she was meant to behave and all was well with the world.

My six charges had dutifully appeared to take their places beneath the shade of the tree, to continue our breathless journey through ancient Israelite history and the development of the book from which all of them except Eric would read a portion in the next few months, symbolically taking their place in the Jewish community by so doing. And I only had four more sessions to bring together the various social, political, geographical and religious factors that had led to the production of that document.

I began with a brief review of the astronomical discussion of the previous day, reminding them of the effect of the seasons on the lives of the earliest humans. I pointed out their perception that when the weather was as they wanted and expected it to be they felt protected and looked after. And from there, I introduced the idea of the institution of ways of marking those special occasions, turning points in the cycle of the year.

'We've already said how the full moon of the first month and the seventh month were occasions for celebrations of the spring and the autumn respectively,' I said. I couldn't get my head around saying 'fall' instead of autumn, so I had decided not to bother any more. They could cope. 'And remember that the harvest in the autumn was the most important time in our ancestors' lives. They had gathered in their harvest, so they were absolutely delighted. And how do you think they showed their delight?'

'By having a party?' suggested Eric. The others laughed.

'Eric's not far wrong,' I responded. 'They've got all these crops, ready to make new bread and new wine – so why not have a party? But they want to do something else as well. What do you say to someone if they've given you lots of good things?'

'You say thanks,' said Alison.

'Right,' I said. 'And how did they say thanks?'

'By having a party?' said Eric again. I shook my head.

'No, they did more than that. Remember, they believed that these gifts had been given to them by a divine power somewhere beyond the clouds,' I waved my hand vaguely upwards. 'And they thought the best way to say thanks was to give some of it back. The people would use the good things they had been given to make meals for themselves. So they decided that they would invite to that meal the divine power that had provided the food for them, preparing it as well as they could and sending it back to where it had come from.' I waved my hand skywards once again.

'Sacrifice,' said Darren, thoughtfully.

'Exactly,' I confirmed. 'The whole point of sacrifice was that they had been given something – flocks or crops – and so they gave some of it back. And they did this by setting fire to it – basically offering it as a 'meal' for God – and watching the smoke go up into the sky and disappear, making them think that whatever dwelt above the skies really was accepting their gift. And they believed that if their offering was accepted, they would be rewarded with more good things a year later.'

'Suppose they weren't rewarded?' asked Eric, in an accusing tone. 'Suppose the next year's harvest was no good? Did that mean that God didn't like what they'd made for Him?'

'Good question, Eric,' I said, deciding not to challenge his reference to God as 'Him'. 'Remember that the people understood very little about their world and how all these things worked. So if they didn't get the rain at the right time or their animals didn't produce healthy new flocks, they figured they'd upset God, that there was something wrong with the meal they'd made. So gradually they decided that there needed to be a special way of communicating with God that was different from the normal way that their lives went. They came up with all sorts of ideas about how their offering should be prepared, how it should be presented, where it should be presented and who should present it. '

'Is that why we have rabbis?' asked Jess. I smiled.

'No Jess, rabbis came on to the scene much later. But there was a group of people whose job it was to make the sacrifices on behalf of the people.'

'Priests,' said Alison.

'That's them,' I said. 'They were the group of people who were chosen to speak and to make offerings to God on behalf of the people. Remember the people were terrified of what might happen to them if they got anything wrong, if they upset God, so these priests had to do everything just right. They had to carry out the sacrifices with precision, they had to wear exactly the right clothes and be properly prepared to meet with God on behalf of the people.

'Let's start with the people. Time for another look at the Torah – this book that you're going to be reading from when you become *bar-* or *bat-mitzvah*. Broadly speaking, the book of Genesis gets our ancestors from the land of Canaan into Egypt, then the first half of the book of Exodus gets them out again and into the wilderness. We'll get back to the second half of Exodus in a minute, but basically it spends a lot of time talking about the special place where the Israelites would meet with God. Then comes the book of Leviticus, a whole series of what you might call religious instructions about how the people should respect God and the role of the priests in that was crucial.'

I handed out the copies of the *Tanakh*. 'Turn to the very start of the book of Leviticus,' I said, adding, 'As I recall, Josh, this is what you'll be reading as your *bar-mitzvah* portion.' A strange look passed across Josh's face; he suddenly sat up and was the first to reach the page. He started reading.

I stopped Josh once he had reached verse 13 – I figured they'd had enough information about the blood and guts of the sacrifice by then. Jess and Julie were making faces at one another while Darren grimaced. Josh and Eric seemed to be enjoying the macabre biblical obsession with detail; Alison, typically, was just staring at the ground.

'That's *so* gross,' said Julie, screwing up her face in disgust.

'I think it's cool,' said Josh with a wicked smile. 'I get to read all about that blood and stuff on my *bar-mitzvah* – neat.'

'You're gross too,' said Jess, moving away from Josh.

'Like I said, our ancestors wanted to be sure that their offerings were presented in a way that would be exactly right. And they appointed a special group of people whose job it was to make sure that happened. Those verses Josh just read for us make it pretty clear who those people were…' I phrased those last words to make them into a question. It was Darren who provided the answer.

'The sons of Aaron?' he said.

'That's right,' I confirmed. 'And look how many times that point is made in those thirteen verses of Josh's Torah portion.' I paused while they looked. 'Four times we're told that this can only be done by the priests, the sons of Aaron. So these are the special people who make the offerings on behalf of the Israelites. Now let's look at how they made themselves special. Turn to chapter 8. No blood, I promise.'

Julie was sufficiently reassured by my words to offer to read the section that dealt with the special clothing for Aaron and his sons. Once she had finished, I continued outlining the various ways in which the priests made themselves distinct from the ordinary people on whose behalf they were approaching God. 'They were a separate tribe,' I explained, 'the Levites. It was their job to approach that dangerous place where God was – a place that was in a different realm from everyday human life. And our ancestors had a special word to describe that realm, the separate place where God dwelt. The Hebrew word was *kadosh* – which we translate as holy, but it really means different or separate – telling us that God dwells in another realm, one that we don't really understand but that we should respect and be aware of. And it was one that needed to be approached with caution – if you got it wrong, you could bring disaster on yourself and maybe even all the people. One more little section to read –' I flicked to the next page to find the place '– chapter 10. Darren?'

Darren read the first three verses of the chapter, which told how Aaron's sons Nadab and Abihu had approached God in a way that was not correct, offering what the Torah called 'alien fire', and were instantly killed.

'That was a bit harsh,' said Jess.

'That's what the people believed,' I responded. 'That if you got it wrong, God would punish you. That's why the priests had to be so careful to get it right on the people's behalf and why the people trusted the priests to tell them what was right and what was wrong.'

It was time for a change of emphasis. 'Okay,' I said. 'We just read about these two sons of Aaron getting zapped because they did something wrong in God's presence. But where was God's presence? Remember I mentioned before that we'd get back to the second half of the book of Exodus, which talks a lot about the special place where the Israelites could meet with God. Any of you know what that is?'

'The Temple?' asked Alison.

'You're sort of right,' I said. 'Eventually that was the place. But remember that the people are in the wilderness right now, having just left Egypt – the Temple comes much later, once they've settled and King David has made Jerusalem their capital. There was a special place they set up whenever they camped in the wilderness called the sanctuary. And in the middle of that sanctuary, that special place that was holy – *kadosh* – was something very special …' I slowed down, trying to introduce some suspense into my voice as I clicked the laptop. They all moved forward, intrigued, and watched an early scene of 'Raiders of the Lost Ark' where Harrison Ford as Indiana Jones explained the legend and the significance of the Ark of the Covenant.

Once the clip had finished, I asked a series of questions to check that they had grasped the information about this ancient artefact that purportedly contained the stones on which the Ten Commandments were inscribed. It had been carried through the wilderness by the ancient Israelites and had, after various adventures, finally found its home in the Temple in Jerusalem built by King David's son Solomon. It was believed to possess awesome power – perhaps that which had destroyed Nadab and Abihu. I also read them a few verses from the second book of Samuel, describing how poor Uzzah was instantly struck dead for touching the Ark when he tried to prevent it falling from a cart on its way into Jerusalem.[18]

'That was harsh too,' complained Jess.

'God sure didn't like people going close to that Ark,' said Julie.

I nodded. 'We don't know what that's really all about. But that tells us why the people thought it was necessary to have a special group of people to make offerings – people specially trained to approach that power on their behalf. Just like Indiana Jones said,' I added. Time for a bit of light-hearted relief …

'Okay, we know that the story of Indiana Jones finding the Ark of the Covenant can't be true,' I assured them. 'It disappeared hundreds of years ago. It certainly wasn't waiting around for Indiana Jones or Hitler's archaeologists or anyone else to discover it in the twentieth century. But let's just watch what happens in the film when they try to use the Ark and the priestly rituals to communicate with God…'

I advanced the DVD to the section where the French archaeologist was preparing to open it and carry out what he believed to be the ancient priestly ritual. 'Look at the Ark,' I said,

---

[18] 2 Samuel 6:1-7

as we watched the incredible sight of it being carried into a cave by Nazi soldiers. 'It's an exact copy of how it would have looked, based on the description in the book of Exodus. And see what he's wearing,' I continued, as the scene shifted to the Frenchman presiding over what one of the Nazi officers contemptuously described as '… this Jewish ritual …', 'he's wearing exactly what the High Priest would have worn – the description we read earlier. Special clothes, special things – but the wrong people – watch…'

They watched as the early 1980s special effects portrayed the wonder and the terror of this encounter with the divine, ending with bolts of fire cutting through all those present. Predictably, Jess and Julie screamed as two of the characters' faces melted, and, equally predictably, Josh and Eric laughed.

'Now we know none of this is true,' I said, pressing pause just as the lid of the Ark slammed shut to seal its terrible power. 'Like I said, we know the ark disappeared more than two and a half thousand years ago. But I wanted you to see that, to get an idea of the way the people perceived the power of God in ancient times.'

Time to move forward. 'We've already talked about how our ancient ancestors were totally dependent on nature, and they believed there was a divine power that influenced nature.' There were some nods. 'And through the priests, our ancestors believed that they could communicate with this power, maybe even influence it – '

'The whole sacrifice thing,' said Darren.

'Exactly,' I confirmed. 'And they developed different types of sacrifice, different things to "say" to God at different times. Let's work out what the different things they said were. Think about the harvest time, *Sukkot*. What were they doing and what were they saying to God?'

'They were prodding the sky, reminding God to make it rain,' said Alison.

'That's right,' I said. 'So basically they were asking for something. They were saying "please make it rain so that we can plant our crops for next year". What else were they saying?'

'They were thanking God for the harvest,' said Darren.

'They were,' I agreed. 'So they were saying please and thank you to God. Anything else?'

'They were having a party,' said Eric, repeating his earlier line.

'You like the idea of them partying, don't you?' I smiled. Eric nodded enthusiastically. 'Well, I suppose that party was a form of prayer – like saying "Wow! Look at all the wonderful things God has given us".'

It was time to tie this all together. 'So there are three different reasons our ancestors would communicate with God. To ask for things – saying "please". To show gratitude for things – saying "thanks". To appreciate things – saying "wow". But there was a fourth type of prayer. Suppose the rain didn't come, suppose the harvest wasn't good? What did the people think in that situation?'

There was a thoughtful pause before Alison ventured, 'That they'd done something wrong?'

'Exactly,' I said emphatically. 'They said please, they said thanks and they said wow. But what do you say if you've done something wrong?'

'Sorry!' came the response from Julie, Jess and Eric.

'And that's the fourth type of human prayer,' I carried on. 'Please, thanks, wow and oops – oops, we messed up and we're sorry – please don't punish us. Let's do a quick experiment …'

I handed out the sheets of paper containing a selection of translated prayers from the camp's *siddur*. The students took it in turns to read and then discussed whether the prayer in question was saying please, thanks, wow or oops. Then they took a vote and pretty much agreed with one another – and with my assertion that every prayer fell into one of the categories of asking, thanking, appreciating or apologising.

'Try that out next time you're sitting in a service – look at the words we're singing or reading and decide if we're saying please, thanks, wow or oops. I guarantee it'll be one of them,' I said.

'But let's get back to those ancient times, when our ancestors gradually began to understand that the rain they needed might be withheld because God was angry with them for something they'd done wrong. So, along with the please and the thanks and the wow of the *Sukkot* harvest celebrations, they realised that saying sorry might be a good idea as well. But not at the actual *Sukkot* celebrations – they were too much fun! So just a few days before the full moon of the seventh month when the harvest would be celebrated, they introduced a special ceremony: a national day of saying sorry. The High Priest had to prepare himself for the most important part of his role – approaching the Ark in the Holy of Holies at the centre of the Temple and asking forgiveness for the people's sins. Remember the film –' I pointed to the laptop, still showing the Ark of the Covenant, alone and menacing in a darkened cave '– if the High Priest got it wrong, they were in big trouble. It was – literally – an awesome moment,' I added.

'So that's why we have *Yom Kippur*?' asked Darren, his voice seeming to reflect some of that awe.

'That's why,' I confirmed. 'Originally it was to clean the slate, to say to God "Please forgive anything we might have done wrong in the last year and be kind to us and make the rain fall so we won't die." The whole point of *Yom Kippur* was to get rid of the people's sins in time for the harvest celebration so they could have a great celebration with a clear conscience, confident that the rain would come. Nowadays we don't place so much emphasis on the need for rain, obviously,' I went on. 'We're not so tied to the land, and – especially where I come from – there's no shortage of rain in the early autumn. But back then – and even today for farmers in countries with that kind of climate – no rain meant catastrophe. So it was up to the High Priest to make sure he said sorry properly on the people's behalf. That was the original reason for *Yom Kippur*, the Day of Atonement.'

'Where does *Rosh ha-Shanah* fit into that?' asked Alison.

'Good question,' I said. 'Remember we talked about how our ancestors used the moon to mark the passing of time – and how the full moon of the spring and the autumn were the most crucial times of the year?' There were nods from my little group. 'Well, they also noted when the moon was new – when it first became visible as a tiny new crescent. That was also a special occasion to be marked.'

'It gets mentioned in our prayerbooks, right?' asked Darren.

'Sometimes, yes,' I agreed, 'particularly Orthodox ones,' and added, 'because it's marked as a minor festival – and it certainly was in biblical times. *Rosh Chodesh*,' I added, 'the start of the new month. And because the seventh month of the year was the most important one, it was announced by the blowing of the *shofar*, the ram's horn. And it was blown to announce to people: "Wake up everyone! It's the most important month of the year. You need to get all your harvest in before the full moon – and you have to be in Jerusalem five days before that so the High Priest can apologise to God on our behalf for anything we did wrong so that God will send the rain after *Sukkot* and we won't all die of starvation next year".'

I looked around my *bar-* and *bat-mitzvah* group, wondering how much of this they would remember when they were in their synagogues – or Temples as they called them here – in a few weeks' time. 'No more priests doing all this stuff on our behalf,' I said, 'and no more wild celebrations giving thanks for the harvest – which is a bit of a shame.' I smiled. 'But a connection with our ancient past, reminding us of how our ancestors used to fear and respect nature and the power they believed controlled nature.'

'That'll do for today,' I concluded, waving them away. 'You've listened well. Thank you. Have a relaxing Shabbat afternoon – and tomorrow we'll take another look at this funny old book we call the Torah with all its strange and ancient customs and laws.'

'Awesome,' said Julie as she and the others stood up, and I suppose she was right. That a bunch of twelve-year-olds were still captivated by what this ancient text could tell them about their world and their place within it was, indeed, awesome.

* * * * * * * * * * * *

The ninth encounter – Saturday night

'Another great example!' were the words with which he greeted me late that Saturday night. I waited for him to explain and discovered that he was referring to the *havdalah* ceremonies with which the various groups of children around the camp had said farewell to the departing Sabbath. 'Ritual that moves and inspires, that encourages reflection and contemplation – in this case about the sanctity of time.'

'But we didn't really do it "properly",' I said, using the tone of my voice to indicate the quotation marks around the word properly. 'According to the rabbinic instructions, there are particular ways of holding the wine and the spices, of looking at and extinguishing the candle. And we probably didn't do half of that.'

I suppose I was actually quite annoyed with him. His spirited defence of ritual the previous evening had left me feeling somewhat aggrieved, as though he were somehow criticising my liberal approach, which was, broadly speaking, to dismiss anything for which a rational explanation could not be found. Perhaps I expected him, a prophet renowned for his verbal assaults on the insincere worshippers of Jerusalem, to be more hostile to ritual than he actually seemed to be, based on last night's conversation.

To my astonishment, he immediately addressed my hostility, even though I had not formally expressed it. 'There is a clear distinction here. Ritual for its own sake, that has become so caught up in its own detail is pointless and even dangerous, since it deceives those practising it. But that is not so say that ritual does not have value. If properly observed and carried out, it focuses the heart on justice and the mind on seeking ways to implement that justice.'

'Okay. Point taken,' I agreed. 'But who is the judge of when carrying out a ritual ceases to be for a greater purpose and becomes self-defeating? And by what criteria is it judged?'

'That is to be judged not by the manner in which the ritual is carried out but in the behaviour of the individual who carries it out,' he replied simply.

At least he didn't say it was God who was the judge. I would have wanted to hit him if he had.

'God is the judge, in a more abstract sense,' he continued, as though reading my thoughts. 'Not as some kind of scorekeeper, measuring the correctness of the ritual against some kind of divine yardstick. Of course, there are many who would believe it is so. But rather to the extent to which our behaviour is influenced by ritual or prayer. A sort of internal register of its effectiveness.'

I wasn't convinced of the existence of some kind of internal gauge that would somehow measure how well or sincerely we had prayed but I decided to let it go. Perhaps in some oblique way he was talking about a manifestation of conscience, though I wasn't sure. But I did know that time was short, the camp would be over in a couple of days and I still needed to wrap up these lessons about the Torah. I had clearly managed to communicate something of his wisdom and insight to my little group of students, but I felt that they still had questions and needed more answers. Or maybe I did.

'But who decides what is ritually correct and what is not?' I inquired. 'I mean, take the *havdalah* ceremony that we just did. A couple of thousand years ago, a group of rabbis decreed that we should say farewell to the Sabbath – and any other holy day – by saying a blessing for wine, spices, and the fire of a multi-wicked candle and that we should recite a further blessing once that candle was extinguished in the wine, acknowledging the distinction between that which is holy and that which is ordinary – that boundary between us and God that you were talking about yesterday. Suppose we wanted to do the blessings in a different order? Or suppose someone had decreed exactly what spices we should use and how much wine and we chose to disagree with that? If, as you say, the importance lies in the consequence of the ritual rather than its accuracy, what difference does it make what we do so long as the outcome is the right one?'

'So many questions,' he said. 'But in the end it comes down to two distinct criteria. The first is the importance of remaining part of an identified and identifiable group. No matter what Micah and I and others might have said about all people acknowledging the one God in the fullness of time, we never suggested that everyone would become like us. Groups and individuals find that path in their own way. And loyalty to a group, its history, its traditions, is an essential element of the human condition.'

'But that's a recipe for conflict!' I protested, remembering the *Tish'ah b'Av* readings of a few days earlier.

'For too long it has been,' he agreed. 'But it need not always be so. And the role of religion is to guide those who recognise its true message of human potential, which is the need to rise above such petty differences towards a greater unity.'

'But each religion is so convinced of its moral and ritual superiority that will never happen!' I raised my voice once more in protest.

'And that is the second criterion,' he went on. 'Proper and effective ritual practice will produce a moral and ethical society. In the end, it must benefit the society in which it finds itself. If religious requirements are at odds with that society, then the religion will not survive.'

'Or the society won't,' I countered.

'A fair point,' he conceded, 'and one to which we must necessarily return. But let us first of all consider the effect on religion of a failure to adapt to the society of which it is a part. That, after all, is the message of Liberal Judaism,' he added, and I could sense him smiling.

'In my day, religious practice revolved around the offering of possessions by means of sacrifice. The intention was, as you have correctly explained to your students, to establish and maintain the people's relationship with the divine power. But there were those of us who perceived that this sacrifice was a means to an end: the true purpose of religion was not simply the ritually correct presentation of these offerings but the requirement that individuals recognise that their responsibility to the divine power did not begin and end at the entrance to the Temple forecourt. They were also obliged to live by particular rules that governed their lives at all times and in all places, not just at the time and place of worship.'

'I understand that,' I said. 'But my question remains. Who decides which rules are effective and legitimate and what are the criteria for making that decision?'

'Everything is decided by human beings,' he said. 'As you and I have been at pains to point out this past week, God does not write books. God does not write regulations either. But God inspires individuals and groups to make decisions that are for the well-being of the whole of a society, based on higher motives than immediate gratification.'

'But there still needs to be consensus,' I said. 'And equally there are individuals and groups – often in positions of power – who make decisions that are clearly not for the well-being of a whole society.'

'I know this. It was as true in my lifetime as it is in yours. But we know – a deep and fundamental knowledge and awareness – when something is right and something is wrong. And in the end, we know also that what is right will triumph; what is good will ultimately prevail. Rules and regulations are established in societies with that aim in mind: those that achieve or bring us closer to that goal will survive the ages, those that do not will disappear as completely as those who sought to implement them.'

'Example?'

'The sacrifice of animals,' he declared. 'An integral part of the worship of the society of which I was part and yet completely superseded in yours. Your communication with the divine takes the form of words and song – often in your own language and with modern musical accompaniment. Burnt offerings are a thing of the past.'

'Not in the eyes of Orthodox Jews,' I responded. 'Although there has been no animal sacrifice for almost two thousand years, since the Temple was destroyed for the second time, Orthodox Judaism still yearns for that form of worship to return.'

'Surely not?' he said, incredulously.

I nodded. 'The Torah contains many instructions about the manner in which sacrificial worship should be conducted and overseen by the priests,' I continued. 'And if the instructions are written in the Torah, then, as far as Orthodox Judaism is concerned, they need to be carried out.'

'Then there is more of a problem than I had previously thought,' he said. 'It would seem that religion is in more danger than I had realised. And as I said, if religion does not benefit the society of which it is part, then the religion will not survive. If religion is perceived – and presents itself – as a series of outdated laws and customs firmly rooted in an ancient past, its voice will be ignored and the society of which it is part will lose touch with its own soul and with God.'

'That sounds like a pretty good description of the twenty-first century of the Common Era,' I said sadly.

'Not much different from the one in which I lived.'

'Then what shall we do?'

'You must apply yourself to the task I set you at our first encounter,' he said. 'You live in an age where religion has lost touch with its true purpose, where it has become little more than an obstinate effort to cling to outdated and largely irrelevant rules and regulations. I have attempted to explain to you the reason for the introduction of these rules – they were a response to conditions that prevailed in my time. Humanity and its society has developed since then; its religion and its rules must change also.'

'In essence, your task has not changed,' he continued. 'Your duty is still to ensure that your students have a proper understanding of the origin and purpose of the document from which they will be reading in a few months' time. They must understand that what they are reading is not, as so many would have them believe, God-given scripture that purports to outline how a just society should be constructed. What they are reading is the result of an inspired attempt to establish such a society two and a half thousand years ago – and most of the rules and regulations that it contains are appropriate only to that society, not to theirs.

'You must encourage them to ask why such laws were introduced, what was their intention and how successful they were in achieving their aim. Then they need to decide whether those aims are still necessary in your modern society and, if so, how they can best be achieved. In other words, the key is not what the law says but what it was seeking to establish or achieve. If you apply that criterion to every instruction, every story in the Torah, you will begin to understand what motivated those who wrote and compiled it – and in so doing you will rediscover the soul of the religious quest.'

* * * * * * * * * * * *

The task for the next day's lesson was pretty obvious: to get my twelve-year-olds to look at some biblical laws and apply a series of questions to each of them to ascertain why they were introduced, what they were trying to achieve, whether or not they achieved it and – most importantly – whether the law was still relevant in our day and age. I toyed with the idea of using one of my favourite films as a basis for discussion about what happens if laws are taken too literally – the stoning sketch from Monty Python's 'Life of Brian' where a man is facing the death penalty for blasphemy, even though his use of the divine name was completely innocuous. Another option that occurred to me was the anonymous 'letter' to radio presenter Dr Laura Schlesinger in response to her assertion that homosexuality was an abomination because the bible said so.[19] But in the end I figured that the best way to approach this was to go directly to the text of the bible itself. I decided to have the Monty Python sketch ready just in case we had some spare time at the end of the discussion. I sat down with a cup of coffee and started to flick through the laws of Exodus, Leviticus and Deuteronomy, looking for those that would provoke a mixture of interest, amusement and understanding. I had the feeling that this might be a long night ...

An hour or so later, I had extracted nine laws that I thought gave good opportunity to consider a variety of biblical situations and attitudes as well as the chance to talk about the relevance or otherwise of such laws. They provided the chance to discuss Shabbat observance (Exodus 31:15), murder (Exodus 20:13), supporting the poor (Leviticus 19:9-10), dietary laws (Exodus 23:19 & Leviticus 11:20-23), personal hygiene (Deuteronomy 23:13-15 and Leviticus 15:19-20, 25), disciplining children (Deuteronomy 21:18-21) and finally the command to 'love your neighbour as you love yourself' (Leviticus 19:18). Exhausted, I fell into bed, confident that the next day's lesson would be a fruitful one.

[19] See p.147

LESSON NINE – Sunday afternoon

'Thou shalt not …'

'Welcome, ladies and gentlemen. Something different today. So far we've looked at how our ancient ancestors tried to understand something about themselves, about their relationship with nature and the power that controlled it. All that is covered in the various sections of the Torah we've looked at so far. But there's another crucial part of this complicated book that you'll be reading from on the big day that we haven't even touched yet. A whole load of laws.

'We're going to take a look at some of those laws today, but before we do, I just want to ask you a few questions. Think about camp and the way it works. What laws, what rules do we have and why do we need them?'

'Everyone is supposed to stay in their cabins after lights out?' suggested Julie. Eric and Josh both sniggered.

'Good one Julie,' I said. 'And we all know someone who has broken that rule!'

'Hey man – do you remember that time we climbed out the back window while the counsellors were sitting outside the front?' said Josh to Eric and they both laughed again.

'Thanks guys – but we're talking about why we have rules, not how much fun we can have breaking them,' I said. Everyone laughed, then I asked, 'If the rule is broken, does that mean it doesn't work?'

'No,' said Darren quickly. 'Everyone knows it's there.'

'And what would happen if it wasn't?' I asked, nodding.

'Everyone would just wander around camp all night,' said Josh, and laughed again.

'And what would the effect of that be?' I kept firing questions at them.

'Chaos,' replied Alison. 'No one would know where anyone was, people wouldn't get enough sleep and everyone would be tired and moody.'

'Good,' I agreed. 'So the rule is there for a whole load of reasons: to let us know where people are, to make sure they get enough rest and to keep up the atmosphere in the camp. What other examples of camp rules can you think of that help to keep things together?'

The discussion that followed was an entertaining and informative one that encompassed the need for a structured timetable for sessions and mealtimes to keep the five hundred campers occupied, the requirement to have two meal sittings and for order in the dining hall and the necessity of safety regulations in places like the swimming pool. The conversation had extended beyond the boundaries of the camp to traffic regulations when I decided to call a halt.

'Okay,' I said. 'We've agreed that when a large number of people are together in one place, certain rules and regulations are necessary to organise them – for their own safety and comfort. The same was true of our biblical ancestors – though they weren't just organising a summer camp; they were putting together a whole way of life for their society.

'Time to work in pairs again,' I said. I distributed sheets of paper to the established pairings: each sheet contained three biblical verses. 'And time for you to do some thinking. I want you to look at the three laws on your sheet in bold,' I explained, 'and apply the questions at the top of the page to each one. So you need to ask yourselves 1) What situation existed that led to this law being introduced? 2) In what way did the law seek to address that situation? 3) What were the likely consequences of the law? 4) How successful do you think the law was? And finally, 5) Would it work or is it still relevant today? If you want, one of you can write the answers down in the boxes.'

I half-listened to their discussions, which seemed animated and were punctuated with laughter – a particularly raucous outburst coming from Josh and Eric. I hoped that the selection of laws I had chosen for them to consider would provide an opportunity to discuss why human society needs laws and also how most of those laws – not least those in the bible – are a product of the society in which they originate. Then we could think about which ones belonged firmly in the past and which ones still had something to say to us in the twenty-first century.

'Okay ladies,' I said, looking at Jess and Julie. 'Let's kick off with your first one. Read it for us please.'

Jess coughed and held the sheet in front of her as though about to make a proclamation. 'Six days may work be done but on the seventh day there shall be a Sabbath of complete rest, holy to the Eternal One; whoever does work on the Sabbath day shall be put to death.'

'Wow, that's a bit harsh,' commented Alison, looking up.

'It seems to be,' I agreed. 'But let's go through the five points. What situation do you think led to that law being introduced?'

'People were working on the Sabbath?' suggested Julie.

'I guess that covers it,' I replied. 'So how did this law address that situation?'

'By killing people if they broke it!' exclaimed Jess, reading what she had written on her sheet.

'Surely they didn't do that?' exclaimed Alison.

'They did,' I replied. 'There's a story in the book of Numbers – chapter 15 I think – about a man who was caught gathering wood on the Sabbath. He was stoned to death.'

'That's crazy!' exclaimed Darren. I nodded.

'And I think that answers the question about the likely consequences of the law as well,' I went on. 'So how successful do you think it was?'

Julie looked up. 'We figured that as we still observe Shabbat, it must have worked,' she replied.

'That's good,' I said, still nodding. 'And would it still work today?' I added.

Jess laughed. 'I don't think many of us would be around if that law still existed,' she said. The others nodded and smiled.

'Okay, good work,' I said, conscious that there were still many issues raised by that particular biblical law but aware that time was short and there was no time to consider what constituted work or why the death penalty was thought to be an appropriate punishment for breaking the Sabbath. 'Let's move on. Josh and Eric, what did you make of the second one – "You shall not murder"?   Pretty straightforward, I suspect ...'

'Sure was,' said Eric. He reeled off his responses to the questions without pausing. Josh laughed as he did so. 'It was introduced to stop people murdering other people. It addressed the situation by telling them not to do it. The consequences were probably that people took no notice of it. It wasn't very successful 'cause lots of people got murdered then and they still do today.' He lowered the piece of paper from which he was reading and smiled at me.

'Yeah but it's still important,' said Darren, 'even if it doesn't work very well. If there's a law that says it's wrong to murder, then at least a person who murders someone else knows they're doing something wrong ...'

'And that's one of the reasons why we have laws,' I said. 'To distinguish between right and wrong. Okay, let's keep going. Next?' Again I knew that we were missing out all sorts of important aspects of legislation, but I wanted to keep up the momentum.

I nodded to Darren and Alison. It was the latter who read aloud: 'When you reap the harvest of your land, you shall not reap all the way to the edges of your field, or gather the gleanings of your harvest. You shall not pick your vineyard bare or gather the fallen fruit of your vineyard; you shall leave them for the poor and the stranger: I the Eternal One am your God.'

'And what do you make of that?' I asked.

'Well there were poor people and the law was to make sure they had food.' Darren was reading from his sheet; Alison seemed slightly put out that he was talking but remained silent. 'If it was observed properly, it meant that those who owned land would leave food for the poor and no one would starve.' He looked up. 'There's no real way of knowing if it was successful or not – I guess not because there are still starving people in the world. But it doesn't really count today because we don't all own fields and vineyards.'

'But we're rich and we can still do something to help the poor!' exclaimed Alison.

'And that's what this law is trying to get us to do,' I said. 'So you're saying that it is still relevant today, Alison?' I continued, trying to encourage her to say more. She was looking at the floor again; she had surprised herself as well as the rest of us. She nodded, almost imperceptibly.

It was left to Julie to pick up Alison's train of thought. 'It means that all rich people should always give something of theirs to help the poor – not just farmers!' she said thoughtfully.

'And do you think that's a good law?' My question was addressed to all of them, and they all agreed that it was. 'Okay,' I said. 'What about the next one?'

'Oh, that's us again!' said Julie. 'Okay here goes. "You shall not boil a kid in its mother's milk."'

'What is that about?' said Josh in a whiny voice.

'Take us through the questions girls,' I said, conscious that this might be a rather pointless exercise.

'My turn, said Julie. 'It's kinda weird though. Okay. The situation that led to this law being introduced was kids being boiled in their mothers' milk. This law sought to address that situation by telling the people not to boil kids in their mothers' milk. The likely consequences of the law were that kids weren't boiled in their mothers' milk. We have no idea how successful it was and have no clue as to whether the law is relevant today.' She lowered the sheet from which she was reading and fixed me with a stare that seemed to say 'explain that one, rabbi'.

So I quickly explained that the practice of keeping milk and meat products separate – one with which some of them were familiar – was based on the fact that this one law appeared three times in the Torah.[20] Then I pointed out that the most likely reason for the biblical law was to prevent the Israelites from copying what was probably a Canaanite ritual involving a newborn kid being offered along with its mother's milk. 'So just in case the meat in your cheeseburger came from the offspring of whatever produced the milk for the cheese, you don't eat cheeseburgers,' I explained, to general disbelief.

That same reaction greeted my explanation of the section of the dietary laws in Leviticus that forbade the Israelites to eat any winged swarming thing that walked on all fours and then proceeded to list those that were permitted. I told them that there were probably occasions when winged swarming things that walked on all fours were the only thing left to eat after they had consumed all the people's crops, and that this situation demanded a change in the law. I wasn't sure whether it was my suggestion that that this was biblical Liberal Judaism or the thought of people being allowed to eat locusts that surprised them more …

The following three biblical regulations provided further insight into the minds and

---

[20] Exodus 23:19, Exodus 34:26, Deuteronomy 14:21.

intentions of the lawmakers of ancient Israel – and some interesting twelve-year-old twenty-first century reactions. The requirement for the Israelites to make toilet arrangements greatly amused Josh and Eric, who presented an image of God walking around the camp trying not to tread in the Israelites' excrement. Jess and Julie took great delight in the fact that boys could be put to death for what everyone agreed was pretty standard teenage behaviour but girls appeared to be exempt. That led neatly into the ancients' terror of blood – and particularly the flow of menstrual blood that so alarmed our ancestors.

'That's gross!' protested Josh. 'Why would the Torah have stuff like that in it?'

'I agree, it's pretty unpleasant. And that whole section of the book of Leviticus has some pretty unpleasant stuff in it. But the reality is that some of the things our bodies do can be pretty unpleasant. And remember what we said yesterday about what happened if you did anything wrong in God's presence? They were terrified of the consequences of upsetting God by being impure in any way. So that's why they came up with laws dealing with nasty things that come out of our bodies. Many of the laws in the Torah are basic regulations about personal hygiene – probably not a bad idea in a hot desert environment. But because they've been interpreted as some kind of divine command, they have all sorts of consequences in our modern world. It's interesting that Eric said that this law, which effectively separates women from everyday life for large chunks of time, has no relevance to us today. It's actually the basis for the way that Orthodox Judaism treats its women as second-class citizens and it's why the development of our religion over the centuries has effectively excluded women. I know that women rabbis are the norm here, but that's a very recent development. The first *bat-mitzvah* ceremony was less than a century ago – right here in America – and there have only been women rabbis for the last two generations. Judaism is a very male-oriented religion – and these ancient laws about menstruation are the basis of that.'

'So many of these laws are either out of date or just crazy,' protested Darren. 'Why do we bother to read this stuff at all?'

It was time to bring this together and make the point of the whole lesson. 'We read this stuff – the laws in the Torah – because it's important to understand what our ancestors were trying to do,' I explained. 'And what they were trying to do was make sense of their world and organise a society that would be safe. And in order to be safe, so they believed, they had to be careful not to offend the power that gave them what they needed to stay alive –' I pointed to the sky and several voices said 'Rain'.

'Yes, rain and sun and protection from wild animals and from enemies and from diseases – all the things they believed were punishments from God that could be avoided if they made sure they followed certain rules. Like keeping themselves clean and ensuring that their camp was pure.'

I paused and looked around the group. 'But there was another aspect of their behaviour that some of the laws tried to address. The way they behaved towards each other. Over to you Darren – time for the last law on the first sheet I gave you.'

There was a rustling of papers, then Darren read the second half of verse 18 of the 19th chapter of the book of Leviticus: 'Love your neighbour as you love yourself: I am the Eternal One'.

'Thanks. Go through the questions one last time,' I said.

It was Alison who responded. 'Okay,' she said. 'The situation that led to this law being introduced was one where people didn't get on well with each other, where there was a lot of hatred.' She looked up and I nodded my encouragement. 'Just saying "love each other," wasn't enough, so they added God's name at the end of it to make the point.'

'Excellent!' I exclaimed, genuinely impressed. 'Go on, Alison.'

'Well, the likely consequences are that not very much changed because it was a bit optimistic to expect people to love each other. And that's still true today, though that doesn't mean we shouldn't try to make it work ...' Her voice trailed off and the confident interpreter of a biblical law faded once again into a timid twelve-year-old girl staring at the ground in front of her.

'Brilliant, Alison' I said. 'And there are other laws like that as well – the one about harvesting your fields, for example. And the thing I want you to be aware of is that in the midst of all this strange, superstitious stuff about rain and locusts and blood and poo and kids in their mothers' milk, are some extraordinary ideas about people treating each other fairly. And all the laws, no matter what they were about, were the result of our ancestors trying to make sense of their world and to organise their society based on the understanding they had.'

I leaned back. 'All the laws they came up with seemed like common sense to them at the time – leaving a corner of your field for those who were poor was as basic as not eating certain foods or sacrificing in a particular way. The Torah – the document that eventually compiled all those laws – is full of instructions that make no sense to us whatsoever: sacrificing animals, killing people for what seem minor offences, bans on certain sexual behaviour and bizarre remedies for skin diseases. But it also has rules that we can still relate to: loving your neighbour, giving some of your income to those less well off – and there are other laws about treating people fairly that we haven't had time to look at, that also have their place in our world.'

'So how do we decide which is which?' asked Darren. 'Which laws to keep and which ones to ignore?'

'Great question,' I replied. 'And one that goes to the heart of our attitude to Judaism. It's not a question that an Orthodox Jew would ever ask because for Orthodox Judaism, God wrote them all – end of story. But the way we decide our attitude to a particular biblical law is by asking ourselves the questions we used today. The important thing is not what the law says, but what it was trying to achieve and why. So when we see a law telling us how to make a certain sacrifice or to kill someone for working on Shabbat we shouldn't just say "that's crazy", and dismiss it, even if it is crazy. We need to work out what was the question, the situation, to which that law or instruction was the answer. So the question to which the sacrifice is the answer is "How should we show our appreciation for the wonderful things we have been given in our world?" And the question to which killing someone for breaking a Shabbat law is the response is: "Why is a weekly day of rest so important to us?" And once we've worked out what the questions are, we can look at the answers our biblical ancestors came up with and decide if their answers work for us or not. If they do – great. If they don't – then we revisit the question and come up with answers of our own. That's Liberal Judaism – and it's something our biblical ancestors did as well – they weren't frightened to make changes to laws that didn't work – remember the locusts? So we shouldn't be frightened to either.' I looked around the group, pleased to see that they were still focused on what I was saying.

'Okay,' I concluded. 'You've done really well, and we have a little time left, so I think you've earned a little treat. Here's an example of what happens when we take biblical laws too literally …' I briefly reminded them of the third commandment, the law against swearing falsely by God's name, then showed them the stoning excerpt from Monty Python's 'Life of Brian'. The scene worked on so many levels – the fact that the women who wanted to be involved in the stoning were obliged to wear false beards (reminding them of the point I had made earlier; namely that men got all the 'best' parts of religion) the absurdity of being punished just for mentioning a name and the pompous stupidity of John Cleese's High Priest. The audience laughed at the deliberately ridiculous nature of the scene, then groaned when I hit the pause button just as the High Priest was flattened by a gigantic stone.

Tempting as it was to give in to their demands to be able to watch more of the film, I closed the laptop. More groans.

'Calm down,' I said. 'That was just a little light relief. But I wanted to show you that some of these laws simply cannot be taken literally, otherwise they're just absurd. Laws about not saying a particular name or kids and their mothers' milk belong to the realm of superstition, laws that discriminate against women or homosexuals belong to a time when such discrimination was accepted. But we must apply our own standards to those situations and recognise that although the laws of the Torah may have been intended to create a just society two and a half thousand years ago, they may not work in the twenty-first century. That doesn't mean the intention was wrong,' I concluded. 'We just have to learn to understand why these laws were introduced and what they were trying to achieve. If what they were trying to achieve was worthy and still relevant to our modern age then we need to emphasise that and find new ways of promoting that aim. It's the purpose of these regulations that's important, not the regulations themselves because they're bound to belong to a particular time and place.'

I paused for breath. 'Now go away, and take care not to break any of the camp's rules in case they decide to stone you …'

The final encounter – Sunday night

'I think you have some explaining to do.' His words of greeting were tinged with anger. It occurred to me that his attitude seemed to be changing – he appeared less interested in what I had to say and more determined to lecture me. And his sense of humour – such as it was – had disappeared completely.

'Who or what is Jehovah?' he demanded. Clearly he was seeking an explanation of the Monty Python sketch.

'It's one of the many names given to the God of Israel,' I explained. 'The name as written in the Torah, with the Hebrew letters *yud, hei, vav* and *hei* cannot be pronounced. Not only that, we're told in the third commandment that it mustn't be said aloud. It's the holy name of God that only the High Priest is allowed to utter.' I paused, wondering if he was going to solve the mystery of how the name was pronounced. He was silent.

'So the rabbis of old came up with various alternative ways of saying this name. The most common is *Adonai*, the Hebrew word for "my Lord".'

'I do know what *Adonai* means,' he said.

'Then you'll also know,' I continued, 'that if you take the vowels of the word *Adonai* and place them under the letters *yud, hei, vav, hei*, you end up with *y'hovah*. The anglicised form of that is Jehovah and there you have a name of God based on a complete misunderstanding of how the biblical name of God is pronounced.'

'*Yud, hei, vav, hei*,' he said ponderously. '*YHWH*. The God of Israel. Guardian of the past, the present and the future.' His tone was changing; he was about to issue information instead of just complaining.

'The name *yud, hei, vav, hei* actually contains elements of the past, present and future forms of the Hebrew verb 'to be'. The Hebrew word for 'was' is *hei yud hei*, 'is', the present tense, is *hei vav hei* and 'will be' is *yud hei yud hei*. So this unpronounceable name of God is a combination of everything that was, is, and will be.'

'Which makes the current translation of that name in our prayerbooks as 'Eternal One' pretty spot on, I think,' I said proudly.

'And this was the God in whose name we prophets of Jerusalem spoke,' he continued. 'It is important that you explain this role to your students.'

'That's what I want to focus on tomorrow,' I said. I explained how I proposed to show another brief section of the Monty Python film that showed various prophetic figures wearing peculiar costumes, carrying strange props and vying for the attention of the people by shouting at them. He was not impressed.

'We were an essential part of the political arena in ancient Jerusalem, not some entertaining sideshow,' he thundered. 'This was how and why I made my speech of which you are so fond, berating the people for paying too much attention to rams and bullocks, and taking no notice of the true purpose of religion.'

He paused, as though recalling his famous performance in the Temple forecourt. 'Those were dangerous times,' he continued. 'The kingdom of Judah was in constant danger. First we were attacked by Syria and Israel because we refused to join their coalition against the mighty empire of Assyria. Then the foolish king Ahaz of Judah called in the Assyrians to save Judah, and the fate of Israel was sealed.'

I sat in awed silence. A history of ancient Judah from the mouth of the prophet Isaiah!

'My fellow prophets and I watched in horror as the kingdom of Israel was wiped out by the Assyrians. To be sure, we had our differences and disagreements. But they were our brothers!'

He paused; I believed I could hear him weeping. 'Among those from the north who sought safety in Jerusalem were prophets and wise men from the shrine of Shiloh. We met together and discussed the situation and realised that we needed to work to preserve everything about our people's past, protect them in the present and guarantee their future. The idea of *YHWH*, the God of Israel, was born. The prophets of Shiloh shared with us their prophecies and their stories in the name of the God *Elohim*; we adapted much of what they told us and placed it under the guidance of the God *YHWH*.' I was desperate for him to pronounce the name but he would not. He insisted on spelling out the letters and the secret remained intact.

'And so the project we called the Torah of *YHWH* was begun. At its heart was the idea of a covenant: a mutual agreement between a mighty ruler and his subjects. But this was no earthly ruler demanding tribute from his vassal in return for protection. This was *YHWH* promising that the people would be able to remain in their own land providing they obeyed his commands and sought to establish justice in that land.'

'Okay, that was your idea of how it should work,' I said cautiously. I could sense that he was still agitated and I felt that any wrong word might incur his prophetic wrath. 'But surely there were others who also had a say in how the fate of the kingdom of Judah should unfold?'

'Of course there were others,' he replied. 'There were the advisers to the king, the military chiefs and the priests, who each had their own positions to think of. How – or why – they persuaded Ahaz to agree to the Assyrian terms, I shall never know,' he said softly. 'But always the kings looked to other more powerful rulers to protect them, instead of putting their trust in God, in *YHWH*. I tried to persuade them, all the prophets did. We wrote, we discussed, we shouted, we protested in whatever way we thought would work, reminding people that neither Egypt nor Assyria could offer them protection. This would only come if they put their trust in *YHWH*.'

There was a silence. I pictured Isaiah and his followers as a group of political activists marching through the streets of Jerusalem shouting at the people, warning them to mend their ways, to implement the laws of justice demanded by their God or face the inevitable consequences. I imagined the scene where he paraded his ridiculously named sons through the streets to prove his point and vaguely wondered what their mother would have thought of the exercise. And in my mind was also an image of a group of wise men, prophets, gathering together to exchange stories, pooling their wisdom and the traditions they had inherited in various locations, beginning the century and a half long task of compiling what would eventually become the Torah. The books we call Genesis, Exodus and Numbers would contain the story of the people from the earliest days of the world through to their arrival at the borders of the Promised Land, pasted together from numerous memories and stories, interwoven with laws and instructions

borrowed from other peoples or conceived and developed by the prophets of Shiloh. The book of Leviticus, the priestly manual, contained intricate details of how the priests were responsible for ensuring the purity of the relationship between the people and their God.

And then the book of Deuteronomy, the fifth and final book of the Torah that stood out from the other four. It was clearly the work of a single individual or group – there were no contradictions or repetitions, no different names of God or other insertions. And this book had more in common with the subsequent books of the Hebrew bible – the books of Joshua, Judges, Samuel and Kings ...

'Did you write all of that?' I asked him, certain that he would know what was going through my mind.

'Of course not,' he replied, and as he did I remembered our earlier conversations that revealed how little he knew of the stories of Israelite history as described in the books of Genesis, Exodus and Numbers. 'But I started the process. I was determined that the kingdom of Judah should not be swept away into oblivion as had happened to the kingdom of Israel.'

His voice fell to a whisper. 'It was terrible,' he said. 'The people were just taken away, carried off far into the lands of the north and were never heard of again.'

'The ten lost tribes,' I whispered.

'I could not allow this to happen to Judah,' he continued. 'But I knew that it would, unless we could convince our people and ourselves that we were different from the kingdom of Israel, even though we shared so much, had so much in common.'

'And how did you manage that?' I asked, even though I was sure I already knew the answer.

'We were the kingdom of David,' he replied in a low voice. 'All the kings of Judah were descended from him – a continuous line. But the northern kingdom was ruled by a succession of different dynasties, with revolution and counter-revolution, constant upheaval. And they worshipped Jeroboam's golden calf,' he hissed contemptuously.

'And you worshipped Solomon's cherubim,' I retorted, reminding him that the worship that took place in Jerusalem's Temple was little better than what was offered at Beth-El or other northern shrines. His own words attested to that.

'Do not dare to impugn the worship of *YHWH*!' he roared. I had a feeling that our conversation was over. Not only that, but I felt that our relationship would never be the same again. It was as though I had hit a nerve, exposed something about his project as he called it, that revealed something flawed.

I got up and walked away. I was angry, but I couldn't say why. I owed him a great deal for the way that our encounters had helped me understand the reasons why the Torah was written in the way that it was, how it was a record of my ancestors' search for meaning and purpose in the world. And I in turn, I hoped, had managed to put this across to my students, giving them some insight into the real nature and significance of the document from which they would read as part of their *bar-* or *bat-mitzvah* ceremonies. And right now I needed to get back to the privacy of my cabin so that I could summarise what we had just discussed and try to formulate it into some kind of lesson for Monday afternoon – our penultimate meeting.

That last thought threw me into a state of panic. There was so much still to cram in and time was running out. Soon they would be leaving the camp, this haven of Judaism, and I needed to ensure that they took with them enough understanding about their Jewish heritage to guarantee that it remained a part of their identity away from this place.

And with a flash of insight that suddenly struck me as I entered my cabin in the early hours of that Monday morning, it occurred to me that this was precisely what had motivated Isaiah and his fellow prophets more than two and a half millennia earlier to begin the project that would become the Torah.

* * * * * * * * * * * *

My task for the next lesson was to paint a picture of the historical arena in which the prophets operated, emphasising their role of guiding and advising kings and the ways in which they achieved this. This wasn't going to be easy – twelve-year-olds and ancient history were not a good combination. But the context that led to the compilation of the Torah by Isaiah and his fellow prophets had to be set out. In addition to the maps and the facts, I also needed to get across to my students the political relationships between the mighty empires and the tiny kingdoms and how these became a model for the relationship between the people of Israel and their God. The plan sounded good in theory, but how someone like Josh would respond remained to be seen. I had the idea of incorporating another brief sketch from Monty Python's 'Life of Brian' to introduce the prophets, but I still wasn't sure whether or not that would be enough to amuse and inspire my students. Maybe I could get them to proclaim some of the more famous prophetic speeches of Amos and company …

LESSON TEN – Monday afternoon

'Never Mind the Bullocks ...'

'Okay guys,' I said, as I handed out a piece of paper with Ancient Israelite historical highlights on it. 'I need you to hold tight because we're going on a roller coaster ride through our people's ancient history. I need you to use your imaginations here to get a sense of what life was like.' I began my quick summary of life in the days of the Judges and Kings of the Bible, explaining how leaders like Gideon, Samson or King David would emerge in response to threats or attacks by rival tribes. We worked our way through several centuries at a lightning pace, charting the gradual emergence of kings to replace judges as the tribes of Israel became more closely bound together.

'One of the key factors that brought the tribes together was their need to defend themselves against other tribes,' I explained. 'Being bullied by other groups of people was an everyday reality of life in ancient Israel - and that's probably true of all humanity and its predecessors,' I began, reminding them of the scene of primeval conflict around a muddy waterhole that some of them had watched in the film "2001: A Space Odyssey". 'The stronger you were, the more likely you were to survive – and if you were really strong, then you might even get to start bullying other people who live nearby. How many of you have ever been bullied?' Alison looked up in surprise. Darren also nodded. 'Or have any of you bullied someone – maybe as part of a gang?'

Jess and Julie looked at each other and giggled with embarrassment. Eric was looking at Josh.

'What does this have to do with ancient Israel, or whatever it is we're talking about?' said Josh irritably, still lying on his back.

'You'll see,' I said. 'The thing about bullies is that they're always bigger or stronger than the people they bully. Let's imagine there are two gangs in your cabin and they're both picking on you – hiding your clothes or taking the food you're not supposed to keep there.' I smiled and so did they – we all knew about the secret supplies that were in their cabins despite the camp-wide ban for reasons of hygiene.

'One of the gangs comes to you and says they'll protect you from the other one. It sounds good – but then comes the catch. In order to have their protection, you have to give them some of your candy and tidy up their side of the cabin every morning before inspection. Then someone from the other gang offers to protect you – but also at a price. Which one will you choose? If you choose one, it will cost you but you'll be protected against the other one. But if you don't pay up, the one who promised to protect you will come and take everything. If you choose the weaker gang, and they get beaten up by the stronger one, you'll lose everything because you're in the wrong gang. And if you decide not to choose either of them – well then they'll just take it in turns to steal your stuff as you have no protection at all.' I could see they were intrigued – a fact that said a lot about the relationships with the ten or so children with whom they shared a cabin. Out of the corner of my eye I noticed Josh, turn his head. He was also listening ...

'And it's the same with kingdoms. Look at the map. Little Israel and even littler Judah were forever being bullied by Egypt and Assyria. And they were always having to decide whether it was a better idea to ask for Egypt to help protect them from Assyria or to ask Assyria to protect them from Egypt. And those two empires – the bullies – were always trying to prove that they were stronger by ruling over the little kingdoms in between them.

'Okay let's try something.

'Julie and Jess – you're Egypt. Darren and Alison – you're Assyria. Eric you're Israel and Josh can be Judah.' No reaction from Josh.

'Right, here's what I want you to do. Assyria and Egypt each need to persuade Israel and Judah to join them. You need to work out what you can offer these two little kingdoms – and Eric and Josh, you need to decide what you need from these guys and which of them to go with. Two minutes.' I lobbed four pens at members of the group. 'If it helps, you can write down your demands and your needs. Just two minutes – so be quick.'

One of the pens lay untouched at the side of Judah's representative but the other three were being used. The two empires were discussing their proposals while Israel, in the form of Eric, considered that small kingdom's needs. After two minutes I clapped my hands and demanded they stop writing or discussing. Five faces were looking at me. Judah remained dormant.

'Okay,' I said. 'Israel tell us what you need from one of these two big empires,' I said.

'I want you to protect me,' said Eric simply. 'The question is – what's it going to cost me?' I nodded approvingly.

'Okay girls – sorry, Egypt – tell Israel your terms.

'Right,' proclaimed Jess. 'We want half the food you have and we'll protect you against *them*!' She raised her voice and pointed menacingly at Darren and Alison. I turned to Darren and Alison.

'Well we will provide you with protection if you give us ten per cent of your crops and a hundred of your men to fight in our army every year,' said Darren, looking straight at Eric.

'Very good,' I said. 'Okay Eric – I mean Israel – who's it going to be? Are you going to ask for the support of Egypt, Assyria – or will you go it alone?'

'I'll go with Assyria,' he said, smiling. Jess poked her tongue out at him.

'Okay good,' I said, deciding not to ask Judah to join the discussion. 'We'll look in a moment at how the decisions those kingdoms made about which empire to ask for support affected their fate. But there's one more piece of information we need to tie all this together,' I said, pleased that five of them were attentive – and I sensed that the sixth was not as detached as he would have liked me to think. I held up a copy of the map.

'How many of you have been to Israel – modern, not ancient?' Julie, Jess and Darren raised their hands. 'Did you go from the airport to Jerusalem?' They nodded. I reminded them – and explained to those who had not made that journey – of the topography of the land: the low-level plain from the Mediterranean that suddenly turned into the steep climb up the Judean hills to Jerusalem.

'And that meant that ancient Israel – on the more level ground – was always getting caught between Assyria and Egypt,' I continued, indicating the map at which one or two of them glanced. 'And Israel, who rebelled against Assyria's protection, was wiped out by the angry Assyrians in the year 722 BCE. Destroyed. Gone. Judah survived, because their king made a deal with the Assyrians but probably also because mighty Assyria wasn't that interested in a little kingdom high up in those hills. But the ten tribes of Israel were taken away by the Assyrians and spread throughout the Assyrian empire and were never heard of again ...' I tried to give my words a sense of drama and horror to reflect the reaction of the people of Judah as they struggled to come to terms with the destruction of their Israelite cousins.

'The kingdom of Israel – and its people – just disappeared,' I continued. I briefly explained the Assyrian policy of taking the leaders of defeated populations into the heart of their empire and forcing them to live there so that their identity – geographical, political, religious and cultural – would disappear, as they became swallowed up by the Assyrian empire. 'Now remember what I said before about if you were defeated, your god was no good and the gods of the people who defeated you were better than yours?' Five heads nodded.

'Well. The people of Judah had a problem. Because although they were a separate kingdom from Israel, they still shared many things – including the belief in one God. So how could that one God have been defeated by the Assyrians? If that was true, it meant that they, the people of Judah, were also worshipping a weak God who would eventually let them down just as he had let Israel down. Big problem. So what do you think the Judahites – that's the people of Judah – did?' I asked.

'Worship the gods of the Assyrians,' said the kingdom of Judah, slowly sitting up. So Josh had been paying attention.

'Definitely,' I agreed. 'But the priests wouldn't have been too pleased about that.'

'The priests were screwed,' said Josh, 'because the God they worshipped had let his people Israel be destroyed,' he continued, jabbing his thumb in the direction of Eric.

Josh was exactly right, though maybe he could have said it more politely. The people of Judah were dismayed by the defeat of Israel and did not know where to look. An explanation had to be found for the failure of their God to protect their neighbours, their fellow worshippers of the one God. 'And here are the people who gave the explanation they needed,' I said with a flourish and turned to the laptop at my side. A few clicks and my intrigued audience was watching yet another clip from Monty Python's 'Life of Brian'. It was a scene, purporting to be ancient Jerusalem, in which three strangely dressed men were shouting at the passers-by, making accusations and threats as they waved peculiar symbols and uttered strange, seemingly meaningless words. The Monty Python parody of the prophets who were a feature of the biblical landscape and, ultimately, the key to the survival of the religion that was to become Judaism, was an ideal introduction to the next phase of this history lesson.

When the clip had ended, I looked around at the six faces, which once again showed confused expressions.

'What was *that* about?' asked Eric. I explained that in those troubled biblical times there had been a number of individuals who had taken it upon themselves to warn the people of the dangers they faced. The biblical prophets were a strange bunch, I told this group of their descendants, who believed that they were transmitting God's word. Like the characters in the film, they often dressed strangely and were usually regarded as being odd, on the margins of their society.

'And yet,' I went on, 'they were the ones who managed to make sense of why the kingdom of Israel had been destroyed. It wasn't that God had let the people down. It was the people who had let God down.' I paused and looked around the group, sensing that I now had the attention of them all. 'The prophets looked around them and saw that the rules that we talked about yesterday – the ones to do with justice and looking after the poor – weren't being observed by the people. The rich were getting richer, exploiting the poor people in their society, treating each other cruelly and dishonestly and ignoring all the things they had been told to do. And so, the prophets said, Israel had been destroyed because its people had not followed the laws that would lead to a fair society. It was God paying the people back for ignoring those instructions.'

I jumped suddenly to my feet. Jess screamed, Julie giggled nervously and the three boys laughed at their reaction. Reaching into my pocket, I quickly clipped on my one-eyed sunglasses and began shouting:

'Hear the word of the Eternal One, you rulers of Sodom;
listen to the law of our God, you people of Gomorrah!
"To what purpose is the multitude of your sacrifices unto Me?
says the Eternal One.
"I have had My fill of burnt offerings, of rams and the fat of fattened animals;
I have no pleasure in the blood of bullocks and lambs and goats.
When you come to appear before me, who has asked this of you,
this trampling of my courts? Stop bringing meaningless offerings!
Your incense is detestable to me. New Moons, Sabbaths and gatherings—
I cannot abide your evil assemblies.
My soul hates your New Moon festivals and your appointed feasts.
They have become a burden to me; I am weary of them.
When you spread out your hands in prayer, I will hide my eyes from you;
even if you offer many prayers, I will not listen.
Your hands are full of blood; wash and make yourselves clean.
Take your evil deeds out of my sight! Stop doing wrong, learn to do right!
Seek justice, support the oppressed. Defend the orphan, plead the case of the widow."'[21]

They were laughing or smiling, but they had listened.

'Hey Isa*i*ah' said Josh, emphasising the middle 'i'. At least he had learned something, even if it was only the English pronunciation of the prophet's name.

'That's that thing you did in our Shabbat service, right?' enquired Julie.

I nodded. 'Yes,' I said, 'and it's one example of many speeches by the prophets, these people who realised that God didn't just want people to carry out pointless rituals and say empty words. Here are some more –' I handed out sheets containing words from the prophets Amos and Jeremiah in addition to the ones from Isaiah that I'd just read '– who'd like to have a go at the first one?'

To my delight, Josh was the first on his feet, almost snatching the sheet from me. He held the piece of paper some distance in front of his face in his left hand and clutched his right hand to his chest and read:

'"I hate, I despise your religious feasts; I cannot stand your assemblies.
When you bring Me burnt offerings and grain offerings, I will not accept them.
Though you bring choice meal offerings, I will take no notice of them.
Away with the noise of your songs! I will not listen to the music of your harps.
But let justice roll down like water, righteousness like an ever-flowing stream!"'[22]

'That was the prophet Amos,' I said in an exaggeratedly deep voice, as the others applauded Josh's rendition of his famous words. 'And here are some more of his words, telling the people that God is displeased with them.' This time it was Julie who took the sheet and she struck a pose similar to that offered by Josh before declaring:

Hear this, you who trample the needy and exploit the poor of the land,
saying, "When will the New Moon be over that we may sell grain,
and the Sabbath be ended that we may market our wheat?"
Making the *ephah*[23] small, and the *shekel*[24] great and cheating with dishonest scales,
buying the poor for silver and the needy for a pair of sandals,
selling even the sweepings with the wheat.
The Eternal One has sworn by the Pride of Jacob:
"I will never forget anything they have done." '[25]

'Awesome,' said Darren. I guessed that his praise was for Amos's words rather than Julie's performance of them. I pointed out the magnificence of Amos's critique of the exploitation of the poor to enthusiastic nods of admiration.

'Can I do the next one please?' squeaked Jess. I looked at the next card in my hand and laughed to myself.

---

[21] Isaiah 1:10-17
[22] Amos 5:21-24
[23] *ephah* a measure of wheat
[24] *shekel* a weight of silver for payment; Amos is accusing the sellers of wheat of cheating their customers by fixing the relative weight of grain and silver.
[25] Amos 8:4-7

'This is going to have to be the last one,' I said. 'But there will be more tomorrow, if you can stand to have one more meeting,' I added in response to several groans of disappointment. We quickly agreed that we would have one final session the following morning. None of them was due to leave the camp before eleven the next day and they promised to pack quickly and meet here after breakfast. All six of them seemed keen to be there.

'Okay, it's Amos time,' I declared. 'Take it away Jess!'

And she did. Oscar-winning melodrama as she screeched Amos's assault on the wealthy women of Israel's capital city prior to its destruction by the Assyrians:

'Hear this word, you cows of Bashan on Mount Samaria, you women who oppress the poor and crush the needy and say to your husbands, "Bring us some drinks!" The Eternal One has sworn in holiness: "The time will surely come when you will be taken away with hooks, every last one of you with fishhooks. You will each be dragged out through holes in the broken walls, and taken away towards Mount Hermon," declares the Eternal One.' [26]

'This Amos dude is so cool!' exclaimed Eric, giving Josh a high five. "Cows of Bashan!" They both laughed. Jess beamed at Julie while Darren and even Alison laughed aloud. A number of people were looking in our direction, wondering what was going on under this tree. I marvelled at the reaction of these youngsters to these ancient words from their heritage.

'And this is what your religion, this Judaism thing is all about,' I said, trying to place as much emphasis on my words as I could. 'It came out of the history of our people as they tried to make sense of what was happening to them – and why the kingdom of Israel had been destroyed by the Assyrians. The kingdom of Judah survived,' I continued in a low voice, 'but not for long. And tomorrow we'll wrap this all up and I'll explain to you what all the stuff we've been talking about at these sessions has to do with your *bar-* and *bat-mitzvah* ceremonies. Now go already,' I said, waving them away to join the rest of the campers emerging for their Monday afternoon activities.

---

[26] Amos 4:1-3

Monday night

'Look, I was a bit unfair last night,' I began as soon as I arrived at the foot of the tree. It was a strangely still night with a clear star-filled sky. An almost full moon shone brightly in its midst. No sounds came from the tree. I sat myself down in the usual manner and continued speaking.

'The lesson we did earlier today reminded me of just how brilliant your insights were: you and Amos – and Jeremiah, whom you never knew but who completed the project that you started as Jerusalem fell. As you saw, the kids were really taken by your visions and they recognised the power of your words as you sought to remind your listeners of the true purpose of religion and their obligation to the God who dwelt within and beyond them to implement justice.'

I paused again, expecting him to say something to acknowledge the compliments with which I was showering him and his fellow prophets. Nothing was forthcoming.

'This will be our last conversation,' I continued. 'Tomorrow afternoon the campers go home and I'll be on my way shortly after that – back to my congregation in England where we speak English properly, and the joke about your name works without having to be explained.

'I'll get the chance to have one final lesson with the children, one last chance to impress on Alison and Darren, Jess and Julie, Eric and Josh the real significance and purpose of the document that was created and compiled over a period of more than a hundred years during a time of great upheaval in what we now call the Middle East. I'll try to make it clear to them that without this document there would be no *bar-* and *bat-mitzvah* ceremonies – which they might be quite happy about – but also no Jewish summer camp and, in the end, no Judaism, the religion that has its roots in the project you started in your day and that travelled into captivity with the exiled people of Judah, allowing them to keep their identity and their hope.

'You conceived this brilliant concept – that religion was a response to that in human beings which is unique: a desire, a need to discover more about our world and ourselves. The ability to create, to love – and also their opposites. The capacity to choose between good and evil, to make moral choices. The potential to develop and grow, to question and seek to understand. And at the heart of that unique human venture you saw a guiding power that you recognised as encapsulating everything that human beings had been and, through their interaction with their world and each other, were in the process of becoming. *YHWH*, the Eternal One, everything that was, is, and could be. Even now, more than two and a half thousand years later, the concept is still breathtaking: a spirit, a moral force that enables and requires us to establish justice in our dealings with one another.

'But we don't always fulfil that obligation. Sometimes – too often perhaps – we fail to listen to that divine voice speaking within us. We choose to do the wrong thing: we mistreat our fellow human beings, we ignore the call for justice and instead we oppress our fellow human beings with brutal indifference. So you created a series of instructions based on your understanding of the divine voice – perhaps the most profound of these is "*v'ahavta l'rei-echa kamocha* - You shall love your neighbour as you love yourself".[27] Three Hebrew words that encapsulate the requirement for human beings to treat each other fairly, authenticated by two more: '*ani YHWH* – I am the Eternal One, I am the power, the vision that has guided you in your past, that guides you now and that will guide you in the future as you make choices about how you will live your lives.

'And then, in order to encourage people to make what you believed to be the correct moral choices, you spoke out and demanded that they listen to that voice within them. Your courage and your words were breathtaking; I'm not trying to belittle the power and beauty of your visions. But when you came up with the idea of a covenant with the power that controlled the universe and guided humanity within it, you established a system that said 'if you make the correct moral choices and live your lives according to what we consider to be the right laws, you'll be rewarded and all will go well with you'. But the flipside of that was "if you don't, then you'll be punished".

'Now we know that some of the ideas about the world in your time were a bit, well, shall we say inaccurate? And the understanding of how nature operated was somewhat lacking – no criticism intended, it reflected the knowledge of your time. So anything that wasn't understood, any phenomenon that threatened or damaged you in some way, say a flood or a drought, it was immediately decided that this was some kind of punishment for something someone had done wrong. And that even extended to political events – a brilliant move. It enabled you to keep alive the vision of God that you had developed because it saved you from falling into the ancient trap of believing that if you were defeated and captured and taken into exile, then your God was inferior to the gods of your conquerors. That's what happened to all the other peoples who were defeated by the Assyrians or the Babylonians at the time. Where are the Moabites, the Canaanites, the Perizzites – or even your cousins the Israelites – today? But you kept the God and the religion, the culture and the tradition, the history and the memories of the little kingdom of Judah alive. If you hadn't, there would be no Judaism, this camp would not be here, and you and I would not have had any of these encounters, whatever they are, beneath this tree.

'But at what price? By setting the whole thing up as a covenant, you created a simplistic notion of cause and effect. It is perfectly reasonable for human beings to grow up with the idea that if you do something wrong, then you will be punished for it. But your system of covenant also creates the converse of that: if something bad happens to you, then you must have done something wrong. And from that moment, religion loses its capacity to be an exploration of ideas and a search for meaning. It turns into a series of ever more ludicrous behaviours designed to stave off divine wrath. And those responsible for supervising those activities become increasingly powerful. The priests and their ilk effectively hijack religion from you, the prophets and the visionaries.'

I paused, finally giving him the opportunity to respond. Still he said nothing. I wanted him to reply to me, to pour out his prophetic indignation or shower me with his visionary wrath. I wanted him to tell me that I was wrong, that the religion that he had guided and inspired was not just an elaborate and sometimes ridiculous exercise in managing and manipulating the human perception of divine reward and punishment. I wanted to hear that it still represented the most noble of human instincts: the search for meaning and purpose in human existence alongside the quest for understanding of our place in the universe.

But he made no response. Perhaps he had nothing more to say. He had passed to me

---

[27] Leviticus 19:18

his insights and his understanding of what he and his fellow prophets had been trying to achieve with the project they called the Torah of *YHWH* so that I might encourage my *bar-* and *bat-mitzvah* students – and anyone else who might listen – to develop a critical approach to Judaism's sacred text. He had reaffirmed my conviction that it made no sense to regard this document as a series of God-given commandments, to treat its stories as though they represented historical and scientific fact. But when I had challenged the concept that underpinned the theology of the Torah – particularly in the book of Deuteronomy, which established the covenant structure of the relationship between his people and the divine power that guided them – he had nothing to say. Did he recognise his mistake and that of his fellow prophets?

But what else could he, could they, have done? If the ancient prophets had not fundamentally altered the people's understanding of God, allowing God to remain no more than a military mascot who accompanied them into battle against their enemies, the people of Judah would have disappeared into Mesopotamia just as all the other tribal groups before them had done. I glanced up at the silent, motionless branches above me, acknowledging the genius of their theological shift that established the concept that defeat and exile was not a consequence of God's letting the people down, rather it happened because the people had let God down. A remarkable concept that allowed the religion and the God of Israel and Judah to survive Babylonian exile and all subsequent exiles.

But now, more than two and a half millennia after that bold creation, it was becoming clear that this vision of justice was drowning in a deluge of human activity that regarded religion as little more than an effort to stave off divine punishment. That was not something that I was likely to change in the one remaining session with my six students – especially as their minds would be focused on their imminent departure from this place that had been their Jewish home for the past twelve days. But what I could do, I reasoned, was bring our reflections on the origins of the Torah to a conclusion by taking them through the process that Isaiah and those who came after him had undergone themselves. The gathering and editing, ordering and compiling of centuries of material, which had been begun by Isaiah and had ended some hundred and fifty years later in the days of Jeremiah, could be re-enacted by my group of six *bar-/bat-mitzvah* students who had spent the last week exploring the origins, purpose and content of that material.

And so I stood up to bid him one final farewell, aware that I needed to return to my cabin to prepare this one final lesson. By this time tomorrow, I would be well on my way back to the United Kingdom, so this was our last night time encounter. I silently thanked him for the way in which he had challenged and guided me, for sharing with me his concerns and his insights and encouraging me to continue to seek for *YHWH*, striving to help humanity become what it could become, by searching for meaning and justice in my society as he had in his own. And I thanked him particularly for equipping me for the task that confronted me as a rabbi with many more years of *bar-/bat-mitzvah* students to prepare for their entry into Jewish adulthood. My role was to encourage them to look at their tradition, their history and in particular this book from which they would read at their *bar-* or *bat-mitzvah* ceremonies, and to watch out for the bullocks. It was their duty to look for that which was empty and insincere, that which was based on false or inaccurate premises and to seek out the true essence of the faith to which they were declaring their loyalty on that occasion.

No response to my expression of gratitude was forthcoming. I glanced up at the moon and shrugged my shoulders before making my way back to my cabin. As well as preparing the lesson, I also had to pack, ready for my journey home.

* * * * * * * * * * * *

As I made that final night-time journey, I pondered the strange silence that I had just encountered. Perhaps it was because the period of history that was left for me to put across to my students – the final compilation of the Torah during the exile in Babylon – was a period of history that post-dated him and so he had nothing further to say about it. Or perhaps it was because I had indeed pointed to a flaw in the theology of the prophets who suggested that political or natural catastrophe was the consequence of individual and collective failure to address injustices in their society. And the consequence of that was to suggest that religion could not withstand the rigours of twenty-first century rational and scientific criticism, which regarded a force that could have guided humanity to fulfil its potential as little more than quaint superstition, obsessed with ritual and custom.

Whatever. That was not my focus for the following day, but rather for the rest of my career. My immediate concern was to impress on my students the panic that was brought about by the Babylonian siege of Jerusalem and the way this experience, and the exile that followed it, was utilised by the authors of the Torah. They sought on the one hand to use the devastation of the kingdom of Judah as a sign of punishment for the people's failings and on the other to encourage them to believe that their heritage was worth remembering and, if possible, restoring. They believed they could achieve this by compiling a document for the people to learn from as they were carried into exile. And my task was to try and do the same for my charges, who were also about to be dispersed from their cosy haven of Jewish identity. The words of Jeremiah had guided the people of Judah on their journey two and a half thousand years ago and that would be the focus of my final lesson the following day.

* * * * * * * * * * * * *

LESSON ELEVEN – Tuesday morning

'The Babylonians are coming ...'

'Well guys,' I said, looking around the group once they had all seated themselves. 'It's the last day of camp so this is our final meeting.' They all looked sad. I assumed that was because they were about to leave camp, rather than because it was our final meeting. They'd all turned up though – I wouldn't have been surprised if they'd stayed with their friends in their cabins, to say their final farewells. The whole camp had an unfamiliar air of impermanence and insecurity hanging over it – almost as though its inhabitants were re-enacting the numerous times that Jews had been made to pack up and leave places in the past. If only all those occasions had been like this: sad for sure, but not accompanied by persecution, destruction or death.

'Let's get on with it,' I said. 'We have to get to the moment where we find out how the Torah – the Five Books of Moses – came to be written, which is the whole point of what we've been talking about in these sessions. If you remember, we were at the point where the kingdom of Israel had just been destroyed and the survivors in Judah were trying to work out how that could have happened – how their God could have let the Israelites be wiped out.' There were vague nods. 'Anyone remember how they managed to explain it – and who did the explaining?'

'The prophets told them that they hadn't kept God's laws – and that was why their kingdom had been destroyed.' To my surprise, the words came from Josh.

'And do you think the people of Judah learned the lesson?' They looked at me, unsure, but slowly began shaking their heads. 'You're right,' I said. 'The Assyrians were overthrown by the Babylonians but the situation remained the same – the bullying we talked about yesterday, the need for the king of Judah to choose whether to follow Egypt or Babylon, the prophets warning them of what would happen if they didn't bring justice into their society. And they didn't,' I added, turning to the laptop.

'More Monty Python?' asked Eric, hopefully.

I shook my head. 'Sorry, Eric. This is a film about the prophet who was around when the people of Judah faced catastrophe – his name was Jeremiah. He was the son of a priest,' I added, by way of introduction to the scene I was about to show. 'He was about to offer a sacrifice on behalf of the king of Judah but he had seen the wickedness of the people of Judah and spoke words of judgement instead of making the sacrifice.'

'Just like Isaiah,' murmured Darren. I nodded and switched on the laptop.

I had never liked film versions of biblical events, but the scene where Jeremiah was running through the narrow streets of Jerusalem, seeing the cruelty and selfishness of its inhabitants before returning to the Temple was exactly what I needed to introduce the destruction of the city. He was supposed to sacrifice a goat; instead, he uttered these famous prophetic words:

'Hear the word of the LORD[28], all you people of Judah who come through these gates to worship the LORD. This is what the LORD, the God of Israel, says: "Reform your ways and your actions, and I will let you live in this place. Do not trust in deceptive words and say, "This is the Temple of the LORD, the Temple of the LORD, the Temple of the LORD!" If you really change your ways and your actions and deal with each other justly, if you do not oppress the alien, the fatherless or the widow and do not shed innocent blood in this place, and if you do not follow other gods to your own harm, then I will let you live in this place, in the land I gave your forefathers for ever and ever. But look, you are trusting in deceptive words that are worthless.

"Will you steal and murder, commit adultery and perjury, burn incense to Baal and follow other gods you have not known, and then come and stand before me in this house, which bears my Name, and say, "We are safe" - safe to do all these detestable things? Has this house, which bears my Name, become a den of robbers to you? But I have been watching!" declares the LORD.'

The use of the name 'Lord' was irritating, as was Jeremiah's American accent, but in general, the picture of a corrupt Jerusalem being seen through the eyes of the prophet helped to set the scene for bringing together the threads of ancient Israelite history and experience to explain how the book we call the Torah was produced.

'Okay guys,' I said. 'It was a powerful scene – Jeremiah telling the people that they could not keep on doing wrong, and imagine that they were safe just because they had the Temple. His words are on that sheet we looked at yesterday, by the way.

'And I expect you can guess what's coming next,' I said, flicking to another scene. I gestured silently to the screen, which was depicting what seemed to be a reasonable reconstruction of Babylonian soldiers breaching the walls of Jerusalem and sacking the Temple before putting it – and the entire city – to flame. The scene was a short one – no more than three minutes – but it was enough to portray the total ruin of the kingdom of Judah and the city of Jerusalem in the year 586 BCE.

'And that's one of the events we commemorated last week, on *Tish'ah b'Av*,' I said, pressing pause and leaving an image of Jerusalem burning frozen on the screen. 'Now let's remind ourselves of what should have happened next. Remember the experience of the ten tribes of Israel at the hands of the Assyrians ...'

'They would be taken into Babylon,' began Darren, 'and they would just disappear.'

'Exactly,' I confirmed. 'And what should have happened to the God they had worshipped – our God?'

'He should have been replaced by the Babylonian gods,' said Alison sadly.

I nodded. 'That's what should have happened,' I agreed. 'And if it had, our religion would have vanished two and a half thousand years ago, just like the religion of the Moabites, the Midianites, the Canaanites – all the other tribes that were overrun by those mighty empires. There'd be no Judaism – and none of us would be here.

---

[28] See note 4 p.20.

'But it didn't,' I said, after a pause. 'And we are here.'

'So how did Judaism survive?' It was Jess who broke the silence. I had no idea how long it had lasted. Turning to the laptop, I clicked on a music track that I had lined up. Don MacLean's voice emerged, singing his version of the well-known words of the psalm written by the exiled people of Judah, weeping by the waters of Babylon and wistfully recalling their home. We listened as the melody faded at the end of the song, and as it did, I read the English translation of the entire psalm, ending with the verse that offered a blessing to anyone who smashed Babylon's babies against the rocks. [29]

'Ouch!' exclaimed Eric.

'Imagine those words being sung to that same tune,' I said and they laughed. 'So the people of Judah were determined not to disappear into Babylonian anonymity, they refused to abandon their connection with their past. But there were two questions that their leaders and teachers had to deal with. First, how could they convince the people that their God should still be revered as being superior to the Babylonian gods? And second, how could they ensure that the people continued to remember where they had come from and keep alive the hope that they might one day return?'

'We did the first bit already,' I continued, then waited for someone to fill in the detail.

It was Alison, after a pause. 'The prophets had already told them that they were the ones who had let God down, not the other way round.'

I nodded. 'Good. But the second question was more difficult and more important. In order to keep their identity, to stop them becoming Babylonians, they needed to know all about who they were and they needed to be proud of their past, their heritage.'

I looked around the group. 'And we've been looking at all the different elements of their knowledge about themselves, their relationship with each other, with the planet and with its creator,' I said. 'So they gathered together everything written or told about them and their past – their ancestors, their historical experiences, their laws and customs – and they wrote it all down. Let's try and do what they did – just call out all the events and the people and the other things we've been talking about in our sessions here.'

I jumped up and moved to the flipchart, which was standing somewhat precariously on the uneven ground. 'Come on then!' I said. 'How does it all begin?'

'Six days of creation!' shouted Julie.

'Good,' I said, writing it down. 'But there was another creation story, remember?'
'The deep sleep, the rib,' said Alison.

'That's right,' I agreed, writing that down as well. 'Then what?'

---

[29] Psalm 137:9

After Noah, we got onto the patriarchs and matriarchs and then we stormed through the Exodus and on past Mount Sinai. They got a bit bogged down in Leviticus, but a little prompting from me enabled them to reel off many of the laws we had discussed a few days earlier as well as the ancient biblical festivals. I led them through the wilderness of the book of Numbers and brought them, breathless, to the start of the book of Deuteronomy, to the border of the Promised Land.

I looked at my scribbled words on the flipchart. It was a mess, but it had most of the highlights of the first four books of the Torah.

'And they gathered all this together.' I said. 'Some of it was already written down, and they had brought it with them from Jerusalem. Some of it had been brought to Jerusalem by those who escaped the destruction of Israel a hundred and fifty years earlier. And some of it they gathered from their own recollections of stories and celebrations, legends and regulations. They organised it and tried to join all the pieces together to make a record of the history, the journey of the people who sat by the waters of Babylon, desperate to know who they were and to return to where they had come from.' That messy handwriting on the flipchart somehow symbolised the collective memory of the exiled Judahites more than two and a half thousand years earlier, without which there would have been no Torah, and no Judaism.

'But there was more,' I said. 'They also wanted to explain how they had come to be in Babylon. And they believed that one day they would go back to the place they had come from. So they had to make clear what was expected of the people if and when they did go back, how they had to behave in order to ensure that this terrible catastrophe wouldn't happen again. So as well as gathering together all the material that had come with them from Jerusalem, they created a new book, an account that summarised their history and their relationship with God. It set out rules for the society they should seek to establish that would honour God and the consequences of observing – or not observing – those rules.

'Let's take a quick look at it now – here's a summary of what's in it.' I handed round a sheet of paper. We worked quickly through the list detailing the contents of the book. Moses' review of the people's journey from Egypt and their encounter at Horeb[30], the brutal instruction to drive out the other nations, regulations about worship, about how the people should be governed, laws to deal with crime and domestic life – effectively a blueprint for an enlightened, God-fearing biblical society. Then came the interesting bit.

'Remember what we were talking about yesterday,' I said, looking up from the sheet. 'When the rulers of Assyria or Babylon or Egypt came to little kingdoms like Israel and Judah and tried to make deals with them.' They nodded. 'The deal they made was called a covenant – a *b'rit*. They had a very simple format. Basically it went like this: "If you – small kingdom – give us food, soldiers and slaves say, then we – large empire – will look after you and protect you. But if you don't do what we ask you, then we will use all our power against you and destroy you." That was how a covenant was set out. There are many examples of such covenants that have been found by archaeologists, dating back to this time – the time

---

[30] The Deuteronomic name for Mount Sinai.

when the people of Judah were exiled in Babylon.

'So the authors of this new book used the idea of a covenant to explain why Jerusalem had been destroyed. They set the scene for the covenant hundreds of years earlier, as part of the history they were writing, because they were trying to give the people a sense of where they had come from.'

'Look at the chapter I've included on the sheet,' I continued. It's chapter 28 of Deuteronomy. It's one of the most intriguing chapters of the whole Torah. Who'd like to read the first fourteen verses?'

To my surprise, Alison jumped straight in and started off: 'If you will promise to listen to the voice of the Eternal One your God and carefully observe all the commandments that I am giving you today, the Eternal One your God will set you high above all the nations of the earth. All these blessings will come upon you and be with you if you listen to the voice of the Eternal One your God ...' She then read the next twelve verses of that chapter, listing all the blessings that would be bestowed on the Israelites as a consequence of their observing God's commandments: abundant food, flocks, herds and children, victory over their enemies and endless prosperity.

'Thank you,' I said to Alison as she reached the end of verse 14. 'The classic covenant between the powerful side and the weaker one. "If you do this, then I will give you that." So what do you think is coming next?'

It was Darren who answered first. 'The list of things that will happen if you don't keep your side of the deal?'

'Absolutely,' I said. 'And look at the length of that list. There are sixty-nine verses in chapter 28 of the book of Deuteronomy and the good news ends where we just stopped, at verse 14. Now let's look at some of the bad news – the consequences for the people if they didn't keep their side of the deal.'

We skimmed through the thirty-plus verses of the most unpleasant details of sickness and famine, poverty and degradation before reaching verse 49. 'Okay,' I said, 'let's look a bit more closely at this. Who'd like to read for us?' All six of them raised their hands. 'Go for it Josh,' I said, to groans from the others. 'You'll all get a chance,' I added. 'Just verses 49 and 50.'

He read: 'The Eternal One will bring a nation against you from far away, from the ends of the earth, like an eagle swooping down, a nation whose language you will not understand, a ruthless nation with no respect for the old or pity for the young.'

'Thanks. Next verses – Julie please.'

She rustled her sheet. 'They will devour the young of your livestock and the crops of your land until you are destroyed. They will leave you no grain, new wine or oil, nor any calves of your herds or lambs of your flocks until you are ruined.' Julie looked up. 'What's that about?' she asked.

'It means you're screwed,' said Josh.

'Something like that,' I smiled. 'No food, no wine, no animals – the enemy gets them all,' I added. 'Okay keep going – it gets worse. Darren – next two verses please'.

'They will lay siege to all the cities throughout your land until the mighty city walls in which you have trusted fall down. They will besiege all the cities throughout the land the Eternal One your God is giving you.   Because of the suffering that your enemy will inflict on you during the siege, you will eat the fruit of the womb, the flesh of the sons and daughters the Eternal One your God has given you. '

'Oh my God!' exclaimed Jess in horror.

'They ate their own children?' asked Darren, not able to believe what he had just read.

I nodded. 'That was what it was like when a city was under siege in biblical times,' I explained. 'I suggest you read the rest of this paragraph to yourselves.'

I watched as their faces screwed up in disgust at the actions of '…the one who is most tender and dainty among you' and was amused at their comments of how 'gross' this was.

'This is disgusting,' said Jess angrily, giving me an accusing look.

'It's in the Torah,' I said. 'Admittedly when this gets read in Orthodox synagogues, it is read in an undertone so no one actually hears it, but it's right in there. The question we have to consider is *why* is it there? Let's keep going – Eric, verse 58 please. Let's remind ourselves what this is all about.'

Eric read the beginning of the next paragraph, a verse that reiterated the nature and structure of the covenant: 'If you do not promise to observe all the words of this teaching, which are written in this book –'

'That's all,' I said.

'That was painless,' he said.

'Do you see the structure?' I asked. 'If you fail to do whatever then these are the consequences… Let's have just one more – no baby-eating, I promise. Jess, please can you read the first part of verse 64?'

Jess read without her usual enthusiasm. 'The Eternal One will scatter you among all nations, from one end of the earth to the other.'

'That's all,' I said, winding myself up for what was going to be the finale of this bar-/bat-mitzvah course. 'Let's just think about the people who are hearing this. They're being told that this covenant was made between God and the Israelites – their ancestors – in the wilderness, as they were about to enter the Promised Land. It's a list of everything that happened to those people and a collection of rules that they should follow once they enter the land. The people in Babylon listening to this are in the same position: outside their land but hoping to get back to it. Then they hear Moses telling the people what will happen if they don't observe the rules – armies will attack, there will be siege and starvation, they'll eat babies and be scattered. And they think to themselves "that's what happened to us!".'

'It was the authors' way of saying to the people that this was really about them. This document they had compiled, with its laws and legends, stories and events, was all about the people in Babylon who were listening to it. They were the descendants of people who had for more than a thousand years tried to make sense of their world, who had lived through extraordinary experiences and come to understand many things about how the world worked and how God fitted into it. At the heart of what they had discovered was the idea that God wanted people to live together in a fair and just society. But, according to the prophets, they hadn't done that. And that was why they had been thrown out of their land – because they hadn't kept the covenant, they hadn't fulfilled their side of the deal.

'So now it's time to wrap up what I've been trying to get across to you in these sessions,' I said, feeling both exhilarated and weary. 'Sometime in the next few months you're going to read a section from this document that these teachers and prophets put together in Babylon. There are those who say that it was all given by God to Moses at Mount Sinai, but we know that's not true. We've seen enough in our studies to know that it's a human document, representing our ancestors' attempts to understand the world and organise their lives in a way that was pleasing to a God who wanted respect and justice.'

I looked around at these young people who were going to be Judaism's latest recruits, inheritors of this tradition that stretched back more than three thousand years. 'And that's what you have to bring to it as well. When you read your section from this document, this book, this teaching, this Torah, use it as part of your attempt to understand the world. Don't just accept everything it says as being some kind of God-given truth – or, worse, reject it and the religion that goes with it just because you can't accept everything. Recognise it for what it is: the attempt of a group of human beings – who happen to be your ancestors – to make sense of this life and to give meaning and dignity to it. The history and tradition, the literature, the prayers, the rituals, the symbols and the practices – they're all meant to encourage you to understand that life has a purpose and that each of us has a contribution to make to fulfilling that purpose. That's what Judaism is – and now it's your turn to take on that task.'

And that was it really. There didn't seem to be any need for fond farewells – and there wasn't time anyway, as they needed to get back to their cabins to collect their belongings before leaving. I leaned back and felt the bark of the tree dig into my back, watching my six students head towards their cabins. Would they remember much or anything of what I had told them? Perhaps. Perhaps not.

'Whatever,' I said to the tree as I stood up and stretched my arms towards the heavens to ease my aching back. I picked up the laptop, then the flipchart. I looked at my scribbled summary of the contents of the Torah. 'I think your guys did a better job,' I muttered at the tree as I walked away.

'Except for the bullocks,' I added with a laugh, not bothering to look back.

EPILOGUE

I had deliberately booked the latest flight home to minimise the effects of the jet-lag the following day and to give myself time at the airport to reflect on the experiences of the summer.

The busy departure lounge seemed so far removed from the countryside venue of the camp that it was hard to believe that only a few hours had passed since I had left the place that had been my home for the past twelve weeks. And there was little doubt that the most memorable feature of that summer was that series of nocturnal conversations beneath the tree.

Did I really have conversations with the prophet Isaiah? If it seemed improbable at the time; it seemed completely ridiculous now. But I had clearly encountered something, of that I was sure. Perhaps it was just some kind of internal dialogue as I tried to plan out what I wanted to get across to my young students the following day. And maybe sitting alone under the night sky in that rarefied Jewish environment where it was okay to dress up as a biblical prophet put me closer to the origins of my religion and whatever it was that had encouraged me to become a rabbi. In the end, I concluded, as I waited for my flight back to England to be called, I would never know. But in the end, it didn't really matter.

What mattered was that I had been able to draw on whatever it was that I had encountered there to provide my *bar-/bat-mitzvah* students with what I hoped was an insight into the origin and purpose of the book from which they would read when they each – with the exception of Eric – celebrated their ceremony.

Would they remember what I'd tried to teach them? Probably not. They'd have their big day in front of their *kvelling* parents and grandparents, they'd probably get to open envelopes containing more money than they'd imagined and no doubt be feted at an expensive reception and dinner dance with too many speeches and too many courses. I pictured Jess and Julie in glittering ball gowns and Josh in a sharp suit revelling in the attention, though it was less easy to imagine Darren and Alison in such an environment.

But maybe, just maybe, the memory of those lunchtime discussions we had shared beneath that tree in California would hover imperceptibly above those celebrations, reminding them of how the book from which they read that Saturday morning wasn't just some peculiar relic from a bygone age. That reading from it wasn't just an unpleasant ordeal to mark this ancient rite of passage but was, in fact, an opportunity to engage with their ancestors' struggle to understand their world and an encouragement to try and make sense of ours. And perhaps they'd look around the synagogue or the banqueting hall, or just reflect once they were back in their teenage bedrooms after it was all over, and remember how, one summer at camp, some crazy English rabbi had told them to search for what this *bar-/bat-mitzvah* ceremony, this religion called Judaism, was really all about: the quest for knowledge, understanding and justice – and never mind the bullocks.

* * * * * * * * * * *

THE LESSON PLANS

As indicated at the start of this book, there are various ways to use its material with a *bar-/bat-mitzvah* class. The lesson plans that follow, based on the model set out on pages 9-10, set out the aims and objectives of each individual lesson as well as giving a suggested breakdown of how it might be presented. Every teacher is different, as is any group of twelve-year-old students, so flexibility and creativity are a must.

Wherever possible, I have sought to incorporate unusual materials to provoke discussion. In the context of this book much of their use is, of course, fictional – six children would not be able to see images on a laptop in the open air in bright sunshine or hear anything on its inbuilt speakers. In any event, the substance of the lessons is not affected by their omission (though anyone who teaches groups of twelve-year-olds will know the benefit of varied material!). All optional materials are in italics and in brackets. There are a number of copyright issues relating to the use of such material, however, so please take care to check that you are not in breach of these should you choose to use these media. Any references to and suggested uses of published materials (video, audio, written or from public websites) are exclusively for educational purposes and, as such, represent 'fair use' of copyrighted material.[31]

One way of presenting the material is, as suggested in the introduction, simply to read through the lessons as they appear in the chapters. My experience has been that the participants in *bar-/bat-mitzvah* classes have to a significant extent identified with the fictional American children, and have enjoyed the opportunity to read aloud. The discussions that appear in the book can be supplemented by discussions in class while the chapter is being read, or once it has been concluded. It is also possible to have a class carry out some of the activities themselves before reading the chapter – e.g. the discussions relating to biblical laws (page 96 ff), or compile their own list of the contents of the Torah (p.119-120).

The lesson plans are set out on the assumption that each lesson is fifty minutes long. Discussions and distractions mean that this is often not practical, but it's a useful structure, which can easily be adapted. Should you use this material, any comments on the effectiveness or otherwise of any of the lessons as well as suggestions of other ways of using it, I would be delighted to hear from you!

Rabbi Pete Tobias
August 2008
rabbi@rabbipete.co.uk

---

[31] 'Fair use' of such materials is based on the following criteria: **(1)** the purpose and character of the use, including whether such use is of a commercial nature or is for non-profit educational purposes; **(2)** the nature of the copyrighted work; **(3)** the amount and substantiality of the portion used in relation to the copyrighted work as a whole; and **(4)** the effect of the use upon the potential market for or value of the copyrighted work. The author believes that material referred to in this book constitutes fair use as detailed here.

LESSON ONE

'So what's a bar-mitzvah anyway?'

Aims:
- To explain the real significance of *bar-* and *bat-mitzvah*.
- To introduce the rabbinic concept of *bar-mitzvah*.
- To emphasise the unique opportunity that Judaism offers its children at the age of 13 years.

Objectives (At The End Of This *Tochnit, Chanichim* Will Be Able:)
- Demonstrate familiarity with the ceremony of *bar- mitzvah*.
- Articulate an awareness of the history and development of the *bar-mitzvah* ceremony.
- Express a sense of the place of the Torah in Jewish history and of their place in that continuum.

Methodology:
(Show the DVD of "The Wonder Years"[32], the 'Birthday Boy' episode. Highlight the key points: the fact that Paul Pfeiffer has a special occasion to celebrate his thirteenth birthday while his best friend Kevin Arnold has nothing, the contrast between Paul's family heritage, as demonstrated at the Shabbat dinner table when Paul's grandfather gives him his prayerbook and Kevin's, where his mother lists the diverse geographic and ethnic roots of Kevin's antecedents.) Discuss with the participants whether they feel that their forthcoming *bar-/bat-mitzvah* ceremony makes them feel special or different from their non-Jewish classmates and friends.

0.00 – 0.25	***Show the DVD or compile list of expectations***
0.25 – 0.50	Discuss the differences between the expectations and the opportunities of Jewish and non-Jewish children as they approach the age of thirteen. Encourage participants to consider the unique opportunity that Judaism offers them at the age of thirteen.

Resources:
(DVD of "The Wonder Years".)
(DVD player or laptop computer.)

*Alternative:
If the DVD is not available or deemed inappropriate, an activity which asks participants to list why they are having a *bar-/bat-mitzvah* ceremony and what are their fears/ expectations is usually a good starting alternative.

* * * * * * * * * * * * *

---

[32] 'The Wonder Years' Series 2 Episode 19: 'The Birthday Boy.' First aired April 11th 1989. Writer: David M. Stern, Director: Steve Miner.

LESSON TWO
'In the Beginning...'

Aims.

- To introduce the Genesis creation story/stories.
- To introduce the 'Big Bang' theory of the universe.
- To compare the two approaches to creation and emphasise that these are two ways of answering questions about the origins of life.

Objectives (ATEOTTCWBAT)

- Demonstrate familiarity with the first two chapters of Genesis.
- Articulate an awareness of modern scientific theories about the origins of the universe.
- Express an awareness of the Documentary Hypothesis of the authorship of the Torah.
- Demonstrate an understanding that asking questions about the origins of life is a basic human characteristic.

Methodology:

Remind participants of the creation story in chapter 1 of Genesis and discuss its relationship with 21st century scientific truth. *(Play Monty Python's 'Galaxy Song.'[33])* Discuss its contents in relation to the Genesis story. Introduce Genesis 2 verses 4 to 7 and 18 to 22. Highlight and discuss contradictions between the six-day creation story and the account in chapter 2. Introduce idea of different authors based on names of God, discuss reasons for asking questions about the origins of the universe.

0.00 – 0.05	Introduce, read and discuss Genesis 1:1-31.
0.05 – 0.20	*Play 'Galaxy Song'*, discuss Big Bang theory.
0.20 – 0.30	Introduce Genesis 2:4-7, 18-22. Discuss and point out that *Elohim* is the creator in chapter 1 and in chapter 2 it is *YHWH Elohim*.
0.35 – 0.50	Discuss the reasons why there are different theories about the origins of the universe and explain that the Genesis stories are not trying to be scientific truth, they are trying to emphasise the role of God in creation and give meaning to human life.

Resources:

Biblical texts: Genesis 1:1 – 2:3, and 2:4 –7, 18-22. + information about Big Bang

(CD of 'Galaxy Song' or DVD of 'Monty Python's Meaning of Life.' Note: the song is in the middle of a particularly gory scene and also contains some sexual imagery – an audio version might be safer!)

* * * * * * * * * * * *

---

[33] 'Galaxy Song', Eric Idle, Monty Python Sings, Virgin Records, 1989

1 In the beginning God created the heavens and the earth.   2 And the earth was without form and void. Darkness covered the face of the deep. Then God's spirit hovered over the waters. 3 And God said, 'Let there be light!', and there was light.   4 And God saw that the light was good, and God separated the light from the darkness.   5 God called the light Day, and the darkness, God called Night. And there was evening, and there was morning, one day.

6 And God said, 'Let there be a firmament in the midst of the waters to divide the waters above the firmament from the waters below it. 7 So God made the firmament, and it separated the waters beneath from the waters above it. 8 God called the firmament sky. And there was evening, and there was morning, a second day.

9 And God said, 'Let the waters beneath the sky be gathered into a single place, so that dry land may appear.' And it was so. 10 God called the dry land earth, and the gathered waters, God called sea. And God saw that it was good. 11 Then God said, 'Let the land put forth vegetation: plants yielding seed, and fruit trees upon the earth bearing fruit with their seed in them, each according to its kind.' And it was so. 12 The earth brought forth vegetation, plants yielding seed according to their kinds and trees bearing fruit with their seed in them, each according to its kind. And God saw that it was good. 13 And there was evening, and there was morning, a third day.

14 And God said, 'Let there be lights in the firmament of heaven to separate day from night; let them be signs to mark the seasons, the days and the years.   15 Let them be lights in the sky to shine on the earth.' And it was so. 16 God made the two great lights: the greater one to rule the day, and the lesser one to rule the night; and God made the stars. 17 God put them in the vault of the sky to shine on the earth, 18 to rule over the day and the night, and to separate the light from the darkness. And God saw that it was good. 19 And there was evening, and there was morning, a fourth day.

20 And God said, 'Let the waters be filled with living creatures, let birds fly above the earth across the firmament of heaven.' 21 So God created the great sea-creatures and every living creature that fills the waters, every kind of winged bird. And God saw that it was good. 22 God blessed them and said, 'Be fruitful and multiply and fill the water of the sea; and let many birds fill the earth. 23 And there was evening, and there was morning, a fifth day.

24 And God said, 'Let the earth bring forth every species of living creature: cattle, reptiles and wild beasts.' And it was so. 25 And God made the various species of animals both wild and tame, and all the things that creep on the ground, and God saw that it was good. 26 And God said, 'Let us make a human being in Our image, after Our likeness, and let them take charge of the fish of the sea, the birds of the air, the animals, the whole earth, and all the things that creep on the ground. 27 And God created human beings in the Divine image, in the very image of God, making them male and female. 28 And God blessed them, and said to them, 'Be fruitful and multiply; fill the earth and cultivate it; take charge of the fish of the sea, the birds of the air and all creatures that crawl on the ground.' 29 And God said, 'Behold, I give you seed-bearing plants of every kind that grow on earth and every kind of fruit-tree for food. 30 And to every animal, bird and reptile that has in it the breath of life, I give for food the green grasses.' And it was so. 31 And God saw the whole of creation, and it was very good. And there was evening and there was morning, a sixth day.

Genesis 1

* * * * * * * * * * * *

4 When the Eternal God made the earth and heaven — 5 when no shrub of the field was yet on earth and no grasses of the field had yet sprouted, because the Eternal God had not sent rain upon the earth and there was no man to till the soil, 6 but a flow would well up from the ground and water the whole surface of the earth — 7 the Eternal God formed the man from the dust of the earth. The Eternal God breathed into his nostrils the breath of life, and the man became a living being.... 18 The Eternal God said, 'It is not good for the man to be alone; I will make a fitting helper for him.'   19 And the Eternal God formed out of the earth all the wild beasts and all the birds of the sky, and brought them to the man to see what he would call them; and whatever the man called each living creature, that would be its name. 20 And the man gave names to all the cattle and to the birds of the sky and to all the wild beasts; but for Adam no fitting helper was found. 21 So the Eternal God cast a deep sleep upon the man; and while he slept, God took one of his ribs and closed up the flesh at that spot. 22 Then the Eternal God made a woman from the man's rib, and brought her to the man.

Genesis 2

THE BIG BANG THEORY

How did the universe really begin? Most astronomers would say that the debate is now over: The universe started with a giant explosion, called the Big Bang. The big-bang theory got its start with the observations by Edwin Hubble that showed the universe to be expanding. If you imagine the history of the universe as a long-running movie, what happens when you show the movie in reverse? All the galaxies would move closer and closer together, until eventually they all get crushed together into one massive yet tiny sphere. It was just this sort of thinking that led to the concept of the Big Bang.

The Big Bang marks the instant at which the universe began, when space and time came into existence and all the matter in the cosmos started to expand. Amazingly, theorists have deduced the history of the universe dating back to just 10^{-43} second (10 million trillion trillion trillionths of a second) after the Big Bang. Before this time all four fundamental forces—gravity, electromagnetism, and the strong and weak nuclear forces—were unified, but physicists have yet to develop a workable theory that can describe these conditions.

During the first second or so of the universe, protons, neutrons, and electrons—the building blocks of atoms—formed when photons collided and converted their energy into mass, and the four forces split into their separate identities. The temperature of the universe also cooled during this time, from about 10^{32} (100 million trillion trillion) degrees to 10 billion degrees. Approximately three minutes after the Big Bang, when the temperature fell to a cool one billion degrees, protons and neutrons combined to form the nuclei of a few heavier elements, most notably helium.

The next major step didn't take place until roughly 300,000 years after the Big Bang, when the universe had cooled to a not-quite comfortable 3000 degrees. At this temperature, electrons could combine with atomic nuclei to form neutral atoms. With no free electrons left to scatter photons of light, the universe became transparent to radiation. (It is this light that we see today as the cosmic background radiation.) Stars and galaxies began to form about one billion years following the Big Bang, and since then the universe has simply continued to grow larger and cooler, creating conditions conducive to life.

Three excellent reasons exist for believing in the Big Bang theory. First, and most obvious, the universe is expanding. Second, the theory predicts that 25 percent of the total mass of the universe should be the helium that formed during the first few minutes, an amount that agrees with observations. Finally, and most convincing, is the presence of the cosmic background radiation. The Big Bang theory predicted this remnant radiation, which now glows at a temperature just 3 degrees above absolute zero, well before radio astronomers chanced upon it.[34]

---

[34] http://www.thirteen.org/hawking/universes/html/bang.html

LESSON THREE

'The animals went in seven by two...'

Aims:
- To introduce the story of the flood in the Ancient Near East – Noah, Gilgamesh.
- To introduce the archaeological and geological evidence for a flood.
- To discuss how and why a historical event can be turned into a myth.
- To re-visit the Documentary Hypothesis with regard to Genesis 6 and 7.

Objectives (ATEOTTCWBAT)
- Demonstrate familiarity with the story of the flood as presented in Genesis and in the Epic of Gilgamesh.
- Articulate an awareness of modern archaeological and geological evidence for a flood in the Black Sea region approximately 4000 years ago.
- Demonstrate an awareness of the development of and need for myths in human society.
- Express an awareness of the Documentary Hypothesis of the authorship of the Torah.

Methodology:
Begin by showing a children's version of the Noah story – any 'Bible Stories' DVD will do (or an illustrated written version plus, perhaps, a children's song will do equally well)[35]. Discuss likely authenticity of this account. *(Play Bill Cosby's 'Noah' sketch.[36])* Discuss how durable the myth is – a story that was written some 3000 years ago forms the basis of a children's story that is still well-known and retold. Introduce map and archaeological account of the possibility of the Mediterranean flooding the Black Sea and wiping out a civilisation on its shores. Consider the impact of this story of devastation – compare with recent natural disasters and various interpretations of them (Asian tsunami 2005, Hurricane Katrina 2006). Introduce Epic of Gilgamesh, compare with Noah story and discuss the different interpretations of a natural disaster. Conclude with brief look at Genesis 6:21 – 7:2 – the priestly explanation of catering arrangements on Noah's ark!

0.00 – 0.10	Show a short children's version of the Noah story, sing 'Who built the ark?' *(Play Bill Cosby's 'Noah' sketch.)*
0.10 – 0.20	Discuss authenticity or otherwise of this story and its durability.
0.20 – 0.35	Introduce maps, archaeological details of lost civilisation and discuss. Consider effect on human consciousness of major natural catastrophes – how myths are created.
0.35 – 0.45	Introduce excerpts from 'Epic of Gilgamesh'. Explain its origins, the polytheistic religion of the culture from which it emerged. Re-emphasise the human propensity for creating myths based on natural events.
0.45 – 0.50	Read Genesis account. Briefly explain how an alarmed priest, worried about Noah's observance of dietary laws, felt obliged to clarify God's instructions in chapter 7.

Resources:
(Video or DVD of children's Noah story and/or picture book account).

---

[35] e.g. 'Bible Stories' (DVD), Video Japonica1985.

[36] 'The Best of Bill Cosby' (CD), Warner Bros Records Inc., 2005.

(Words and music to 'Who built the ark?')
('Noah' sketches by Bill Cosby (CD).)
Maps of eastern Mediterranean, archaeological accounts of Black Sea flood
(e.g. www.religioustolerance.org/ev_noah.htm)
Excerpts from Gilgamesh epic (examples printed here, see also website from which these
are taken: www.answersingenesis.org/docs2004/0329gilgamesh.asp)
Biblical text: Genesis 6:9 – 7:5

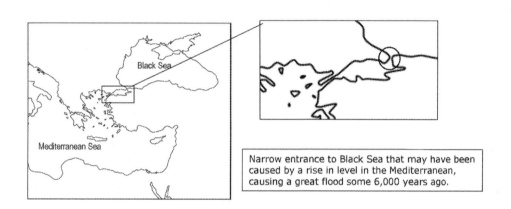

Narrow entrance to Black Sea that may have been caused by a rise in level in the Mediterranean, causing a great flood some 6,000 years ago.

The Epic of Gilgamesh (excerpts)

The council of the gods decided to flood the whole earth to destroy mankind. But Ea, the god who made man, warned Utnapishtim, from Shuruppak, a city on the banks of the Euphrates, and told him to build an enormous boat:

'O man of Shuruppak, son of Ubartutu:
Tear down the house and build a boat!
Abandon wealth and seek living beings!
Spurn possessions and keep alive living beings!
Make all living beings go up into the boat.
The boat which you are to build,
its dimensions must measure equal to each other:
its length must correspond to its width.'

Utnapishtim obeyed:

'One (whole) acre was her floor space, (660' X 660')
Ten dozen cubits the height of each of her walls,
Ten dozen cubits each edge of the square deck.
I laid out the shape of her sides and joined her together.
I provided her with six decks,
Dividing her (thus) into seven parts.' ...

Utnapishtim sealed his ark with pitch took all the kinds of vertebrate animals, and his family members, plus some other humans. Shamash the sun god showered down loaves of bread and rained down wheat. Then the flood came, so fierce that:

'The gods were frightened by the flood,
and retreated, ascending to the heaven of Anu.
The gods were cowering like dogs, crouching by the outer wall.
Ishtar shrieked like a woman in childbirth,

the sweet-voiced Mistress of the Gods wailed:
"The olden days have alas turned to clay,
because I said evil things in the Assembly of the Gods!
How could I say evil things in the Assembly of the Gods,
ordering a catastrophe to destroy my people!!
No sooner have I given birth to my dear people
than they fill the sea like so many fish!"
The gods—those of the Anunnaki—were weeping with her,
the gods humbly sat weeping, sobbing with grief(?),
their lips burning, parched with thirst.'

However, the flood was relatively short:

'Six days and seven nights
came the wind and flood, the storm flattening the land.
When the seventh day arrived, the storm was pounding,
the flood was a war—struggling with itself like a woman
writhing (in labour).'

Then the ark lodged on Mt Nisir (or Nimush), almost 500 km (300 miles) from Mt Ararat. Utnapishtim sent out a dove then a swallow, but neither could find land, so returned. Then he sent out a raven, which didn't return. So he released the animals and sacrificed a lamb.

* * * * * * * * * * * *

These are the generations of Noah: Noah was a righteous and upright man of his generation who walked with God. And Noah had three sons: Shem, Ham and Japheth. And the earth sinned before God for it was full of violence. And God saw how wicked the earth had become because the ways of the people on it were corrupt. And God said to Noah 'I have decided to put an end to all flesh: as the world is full of violence because of them, I intend to destroy the world. Make yourself an ark of gopher wood, build rooms inside it and cover it with tar and pitch, inside and out. And this is how you shall make it: three hundred cubits long, fifty cubits wide and thirty cubits high. You shall make a roof for it and construct the ark to within a cubit of the roof. Put a door on one side of the ark and make three separate decks. For I am going to bring a flood upon the earth to destroy all living flesh, all creatures beneath the heavens with the breath of life in them - everything on earth will perish. But I will establish my covenant with you: you will go into the ark, you and your sons, your wife and their wives. And of every living creature you shall take two - one male and one female - and bring them with you into the ark. Two of each kind of the birds of the heavens and the creatures that move along the ground shall come with you in order to survive. And gather up enough food for you and for the animals.' And Noah did just what God had commanded him to do.

And the Eternal One said to Noah 'Go into the ark, you and all your household. For I have seen that you are the only righteous one of this generation. Take with you seven pairs of every kind of clean animal - male and female - and of the animals that are unclean, take two: one male, one female. And also take seven pairs of every kind of bird of the heavens - male and female - so that all the different species will survive on the earth.'

Genesis 6:9-7:3

LESSON FOUR

'Tell us a story'

Aims:
- To introduce the characters and content of some of the key Genesis stories.
- To reinforce the idea of the role of myths as a basis of identity.
- To consider the intended message or purpose of some Genesis stories.
- To consider the significance of the Torah blessings.

Objectives (ATEOTTCWBAT)
- Demonstrate an awareness of some key characters in the book of Genesis and their associated stories.
- Articulate an understanding of the purpose and intention of such stories.
- Demonstrate an awareness of the importance of storytelling in biblical times.
- To practice and discuss the blessings before and after the Torah reading.

Methodology:
Read and discuss various stories in the book of Genesis. In order to vary the lesson, excerpts from DVDs could be shown to illustrate, say, the binding of Isaac[37] and/or parts of the Joseph story (but there's no harm in just doing text for a change!). This list can be varied and some elements omitted if time is short.
- Abraham leaving Haran (12:1-9 – also mention the idols *midrash* to emphasise different levels of storytelling).
- The *Akedah* – the binding of Isaac (22:1-19 – discuss child sacrifice).
- Rebekah meets Isaac – Genesis 24.
- Joseph's dreams, their fulfilment and Jacob going to Egypt (37:1-28, 42:1-9, 46:2-7 (or an alternative version). Explain that the purpose of this whole story is to get the Israelites to Egypt in order for the Exodus to take place).

0.00 – 0.10	Practice Torah blessings. Discuss weight of the phrase *torat emet* – true instruction.
0.10 – 0.20	The binding of Isaac – child sacrifice in Canaanite society.
0.20 – 0.30	Isaac, Rekekah and the camel …
0.30 – 0.45	The Joseph stories and their purpose.
0.45 – 0.50	Conclusion: what is the purpose and intention of these legends? How 'true' are they likely to be?

Resources:
Biblical texts (easier to have complete editions of *Tanakh*).
DVD or other versions of stories for variety and means to play them (optional).

* * * * * * * * * * * *

---

[37] e.g. 'Abraham and Isaac' (DVD), Boulevard Entertainment 2006

LESSON FIVE

'Let my people go!'

Aims:
- To introduce and re-evaluate the story of the Exodus from Egypt.
- To introduce the archaeological and geological evidence for a volcanic eruption at the time of the Exodus.
- To consider how this may have affected the events of the Exodus.
- To consider how and why a historical event can be turned into a myth.

Objectives (ATEOTTCWBAT)
- Demonstrate awareness of the possibility of a volcanic eruption being the source of the events of the Exodus.
- Articulate an understanding of why this event became so mythologised in ancient Israelite culture.
- Demonstrate an awareness of the development of oral traditions in ancient societies.
- Express a sense of how oral traditions can exaggerate and distort historical facts – but that facts still underpin such accounts.

Methodology:
Begin by reminding participants of the Exodus story: the Israelites as slaves, Moses challenging Pharaoh, the ten plagues, the crossing of the sea and the drowning of the Egyptians. Introduce the volcano theory and the recorded details of plagues 1-9 and the Sea of Reeds (tsunami?) as a consequence of a volcanic eruption. Discuss tenth plague – Canaanite practice of sacrificing firstborn, including children. Mention story of Abraham and the binding of Isaac as a parable to dissuade ancient Israelites from child sacrifice. The escape: divine intervention or human opportunism? Impossibility of biblical numbers being accurate – re-emphasise the oral tradition and the development of myths.

0.00 – 0.10	Brainstorm facts about the biblical account of the Exodus.
0.10 – 0.15	Discuss authenticity or otherwise of this story.
0.15 – 0.30	Introduce idea of volcanic eruption and compare consequences to the plagues.
0.30 – 0.35	Discuss tenth plague. Explain Canaanite practices and Israelite propensity for emulating Canaanites.
0.35 – 0.50	Discussion about 'truth' of Exodus: oral transmission of story, reality that lies at the heart of the myth: what was divine role in this event and what were its consequences?

Resources:
Flip chart and pens.
Copies of *Tanakh* (if needed for reference)

* * * * * * * * * * * *

LESSON SIX

'Encountering God'

Aims:
- To introduce the concept of divine revelation.
- To consider the events described in Exodus 19, their 'authenticity' and their effect.
- To consider other revelations that appear in the Hebrew bible.
- To consider ways in which God 'speaks' to human beings and how human beings deal with and respond to this.

Objectives (ATEOTTCWBAT)
- Demonstrate knowledge of the events surrounding the account of the revelation at Mount Sinai in Exodus chapter 19.
- Demonstrate an awareness of other examples of divine revelation in the *Tanakh* and in other cultures and traditions.
- Express a sense of how human beings can experience divine inspiration.

Methodology:
Begin by reading Exodus chapter 19. Discuss its contents, what do participants think actually happened? (*Show opening scene ('The Dawn of Man') from '2001: A Space Odyssey.'*[38] *Discuss.*) Introduce other biblical accounts of divine revelation: Jacob's dream (Genesis 28:10-22), Moses at the burning bush (Exodus 3), Isaiah in the Temple (Isaiah 6), Elijah in the wilderness (I Kings 19: 8-14). Ask children in groups to consider the various revelations.

0.00 – 0.15	Read and discuss Exodus 19.
0.15 – 0.25	*(Show excerpt from '2001: A Space Odyssey.')*
0.25 – 0.30	Discuss how human beings receive inspiration and its possible source(s).
0.30 – 0.45	Read and discuss revelations of Jacob, Moses, Isaiah and Elijah.
0.45 – 0.50	Discuss incidence and effect of 'divine revelation.'

Resources:
Copies of *Tanakh*
(*DVD of '2001: A Space Odyssey.'*
DVD player or laptop computer.)

(*If the DVD of '2001 A Space Odyssey' is unavailable or not deemed appropriate, a longer discussion of the various revelations could take its place.*)

* * * * * * * * * * * *

---

[38] '2001:A Space Odyssey' (DVD), directed by Stanley Kubrick, Turner Entertainment Co. 1968 and Warner Home Video.

ENCOUNTERING GOD

The Israelites at Mount Sinai

On the morning of the third day there was thunder and lightning, a thick cloud hung over the mountain, and there was a very loud trumpet blast. All the people in the camp trembled. Then Moses led the people out of the camp to meet with God, and they stood at the foot of the mountain. Mount Sinai was covered with smoke, because the Eternal One had descended on it in fire. The smoke billowed up from it like smoke from a furnace, the whole mountain trembled violently, and the sound of the trumpet grew louder and louder. Then Moses spoke and the voice of God answered him. The Eternal One came down onto the top of Mount Sinai and called Moses to the top of the mountain. And Moses went up.

(The Ten Commandments – Exodus 20:1-14)

When the people saw the thunder and lightning and heard the trumpet and saw the mountain in smoke, they trembled with fear. They stayed at a distance and said to Moses, 'You speak to us and we will listen. But do not have God speak to us or we will die'. Moses said to the people, 'Do not be afraid. God has come to test you, so that the fear of God will be with you to keep you from sinning'. The people remained at a distance, while Moses approached the thick darkness where God was.

Exodus 19:16-20; 20: 15-18

Elijah at Mount Horeb

So Elijah got up and ate and drank. Strengthened by the food, he travelled for forty days and forty nights until he reached the mountain of God at Horeb. There he went into a cave and spent the night. And the word of the Eternal One came to him: 'What are you doing here, Elijah'? He replied, 'I have tried my hardest to do the will of the Eternal One. The Israelites have rejected Your covenant, broken down your altars, and put your prophets to death with the sword. I am the only one left, and now they are trying to kill me too'. The Eternal One said, 'Go out and stand on the mountain in the presence of the Eternal One, for God is about to pass by'. Then a great and powerful wind tore the mountains apart and shattered the rocks, but God was not in the wind. After the wind there was an earthquake, but God was not in the earthquake. After the earthquake came a fire, but God was not in the fire. And after the fire came a still small voice. When Elijah heard it, he pulled his cloak over his face and went out and stood at the mouth of the cave. Then a voice said to him, 'What are you doing here, Elijah'? He replied, 'I have tried my hardest to do the will of the Eternal One. The Israelites have rejected Your covenant, broken down your altars, and put your prophets to death with the sword. I am the only one left, and now they are trying to kill me too'. The Eternal One said to him, 'Go back the way you came...'

1 Kings 19:8-15

Jacob's dream

Jacob left Beersheba and went towards Haran. When he reached a certain place, he stopped for the night because the sun had set. Taking one of the stones there, he put it under his head and he went to sleep in that place. He dreamt there was a ladder standing on the earth, with its top reaching to heaven, and there were angels of God going up and down it. The Eternal One stood at the top and said: 'I am the Eternal One, the God of your father Abraham and the God of Isaac. The land that you are lying on I will give to you and your descendants. Your descendants will be like the dust of the earth, and you will spread out to the west and to the east, to the north and to the south, and all peoples on earth will be blessed through you and your descendants. I will be with you and will watch over you wherever you go, and I will bring you back to this land. I will not leave you until I have done what I have promised you'. When Jacob awoke from his sleep, he thought, 'Surely the Eternal One is in this place, and I did not know it'.

Genesis 28:10-16

Isaiah's vision in the Temple

In the year that King Uzziah died, I saw the Eternal One sitting on a throne, high and exalted, and the train of God's robe filled the temple. Above there were seraphim, each with six wings. With two wings they covered their faces, with two they covered their feet, and with two they were flying. And they were calling to one another:

'Holy, holy, holy is the Eternal One of Hosts; the whole earth is full of God's glory'.

At the sound of their voices the doorposts and thresholds shook and the temple was filled with smoke. 'Woe am I!' I cried. 'I am ruined! For I am a man of unclean lips, and I live among a people of unclean lips, and my eyes have seen the Ruler, the Eternal One of Hosts.' Then one of the seraphim flew to me with a live coal in his hand, which he had taken with tongs from the altar. With it he touched my mouth and said, 'See, this has touched your lips; your guilt is taken away and your sin atoned for'. Then I heard the voice of the Eternal One saying, 'Whom shall I send? And who will go for us?' And I said, 'Here am I. Send me!'

Isaiah 6:1-8

Moses and the burning bush

Now Moses was tending the flock of Jethro his father-in-law, the priest of Midian, and he led the flock beyond the wilderness and came to Horeb, the mountain of God. There the angel of the Eternal One appeared to him in flames of fire from within a bush. Moses saw that although the bush was on fire it was not consumed. So Moses thought, 'I will turn aside and look at this great sight — why the bush is not consumed.' When the Eternal One saw that he had gone over to look, God called to him from within the bush: 'Moses! Moses!' And Moses said, 'Here I am'. 'Do not come any closer,' said God. 'Take your sandals from your feet, for the ground on which you are standing is holy ground'. Then God said, 'I am the God of your father, the God of Abraham, the God of Isaac and the God of Jacob.' At this, Moses hid his face, because he was afraid to look at God. The Eternal One said, 'I have indeed seen the misery of my people in Egypt. I have heard them crying out because of their taskmasters, and I know of their suffering. And I have come down to rescue them from the hand of the Egyptians and to bring them out of this land to a good and extensive land, a land flowing with milk and honey, the place where the Canaanites, Hittites, Amorites, Perizzites, Hivites and Jebusites dwell. Now go, I am sending you to Pharaoh and you will bring my people the Children of Israel out of Egypt.' And Moses said to God 'Who am I that I should go to Pharaoh and that I should bring the Children of Israel out of Egypt?' And God said 'Because I will be with you and this will be the sign that I have sent you to bring the people out of Egypt to serve God at this mountain.' And Moses said to God 'You want me to go to the Children of Israel and say to them "The God of your ancestors has sent me to you?" They will ask me "What is the name of this God?" What shall I say to them?' And God said to Moses 'eh'yeh asher eh'yeh - I shall be whatever I shall be. You shall say to the Children of Israel that eh'yeh has sent you.'

Exodus 3:1-14

LESSON SEVEN

'Experiencing God'

Aims:
- To introduce the astronomical and meteorological realities of life on earth and their consequences for human beings.
- To contemplate aspects of life that created uncertainty and even terror in the minds of our ancient ancestors.
- To consider human dependence on nature.
- To consider the human perception of divine influence on the world.
- To explain the ancient agricultural origins of the Jewish festivals.

Objectives (ATEOTTCWBAT)
- Demonstrate knowledge of the cycle of the seasons based on earth's rotation around the sun and the measurement of time based on the moon orbiting the earth.
- Demonstrate an awareness of how this would affect and influence the earliest human beings.
- Demonstrate an awareness of human vulnerability and dependence on nature.
- Express an awareness of the agricultural roots of the festival of *Sukkot* and its relationship with *Pesach*.

Methodology:
A good old bit of 'chalk and talk' here (or its modern equivalent – flipchart or whiteboard and pen or Powerpoint presentation). Diagrams of earth's rotation of the sun showing the seasons, phases of the moon, position of the sun on the horizon – all attached. Ask questions and discuss how the seasons influenced and affected all humanity and in particular our ancient Israelite ancestors and how they developed a system of communicating with the divine power at key times in the calendar.

0.00 – 0.50   Presentation of various diagrams, question and answer, discussion.

Resources:
Flip chart and pens (or equivalent) and/or diagrams of earth's rotation, lunar orbit and position of the sun.

* * ** * * * * * * * *

THE SEASONS OF THE YEAR

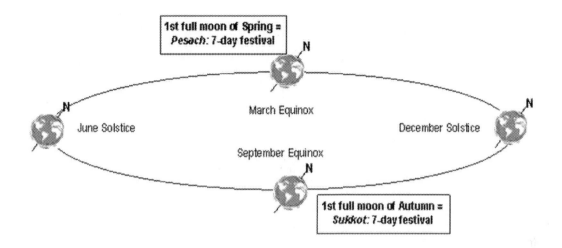

1st full moon of Spring =
Pesach: 7-day festival

N

March Equinox

June Solstice

December Solstice

September Equinox

N

1st full moon of Autumn =
Sukkot: 7-day festival

THE PHASES OF THE MOON

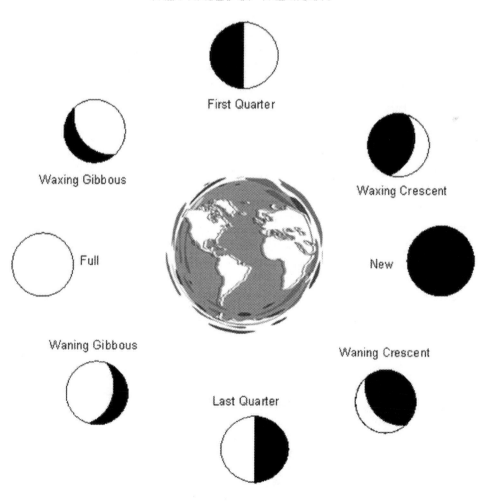

First Quarter

Waxing Gibbous

Waxing Crescent

Full

New

Waning Gibbous

Waning Crescent

Last Quarter

LESSON EIGHT

'Talking to God'

Aims

- To consider ways in which human beings sought to establish communication with that perceived divine influence.
- To consider the role of priests and 'holy' places in that communication.
- To consider the origin and perceived purpose of sacrifice.
- To identify the four different types of human prayer (petitionary, thanksgiving, doxological and penitential).
- To explain the origin and intention of the observance of *Yom Kippur, Rosh ha-Shanah* and their connection with *Sukkot.*

Objectives (ATEOTTCWBAT)

- Articulate an understanding of why this dependence was the basis for the development of religion and prayer, including the building of 'holy' places and the offering of sacrifices.
- Describe the four types of human prayer ('please, thanks, wow and oops').
- Express an awareness of the purpose of the Day of Atonement in ancient Israelite religion.

Methodology:

Review of early human dependence on nature followed by discussion about how they perceived divine influence in their lives. Consider the nature of 'holiness' – special places, special times, special costumes. Introduce the concept of priests taking responsibility for communicating with the divine power on people's behalf – read Leviticus 1 and discuss sacrifice. Refer to Leviticus 10:1-3 (death of Nadab and Abhiu) 2 Samuel 6:1-7 (death of Uzzah); talk about our ancestors' fear of the divine power (attached). *(Show excerpts from 'Raiders of the Lost Ark[39]' to introduce place of religious icons and need for priests).* Introduce four different types of prayer and differentiate between them. Discuss prayer types. Emphasise the 'sorry' part of prayer and establish connection between the yearning for rain and the sense that it might be withheld as punishment, requiring the need to say sorry. Introduce idea of *Yom Kippur* in this context.

0.00 – 0.05	Review of ancient Israelite dependence on nature and the festivals of *Sukkot* and *Pesach* – particularly the need for rain at *Sukkot* time.
0.05 – 0.15	Discuss observance of these festivals – the Israelites gathering at 'high places'; eventually the Temple in Jerusalem overseen by priests. Look at Leviticus chapter 1, discuss place of sacrifice in religion.
0.15 – 0.35	The fear of getting it wrong – Leviticus 10:1-9, 2 Samuel 6, ('Raiders of the Lost Ark').
0.35 – 0.45	Discuss different types of human prayer: please, thanks, wow or oops.
0.45 – 0.50	Conclude: refer back to the need for rain and discuss the idea that rain might be withheld as punishment, requiring the need for an apology: *Yom Kippur.* Emphasise the connection between *Sukkot, Yom Kippur* and *Rosh ha-Shanah.*

Resources:

Diagrams from previous lesson as reminders.

---

[39] 'Raiders of the Lost Ark' (DVD), directed by Steven Spielberg, Paramount Pictures, Lucasfilm 1981.

Copies of *Tanakh.*
('Raiders of the Lost Ark' DVD and laptop.)

And Nadab and Abihu, the sons of Aaron, each took their fire-pans and placed in them alien fire which God had not requested of them, and they approached the presence of the Eternal One. And fire came out from before the Eternal One and consumed them, and they perished before the Eternal One. And Moses said to Aaron 'This is what the Eternal One meant by the words 'I will be sanctified by those who approach Me and I will be honoured by all the people.' And Aaron was silent.

Leviticus 10:1-3

And David gathered together all the men of Israel, thirty thousand men and all of them went up from Ba'alei Y'hudah to bring up the ark of God that was called by the name: the name of the Eternal One of Hosts who dwelt between the cherubim that were on it. The ark was transported on a newly built wagon, which was brought out of the house of Abinadav who lived in Gibe'ah. Uzzah and Ahio, sons of Abinadav, steered the new wagon. And the ark of God was brought out from the house of Abinadav in Gibe'ah with Ahio leading it. And David and the whole House of Israel played all kinds of wooden instruments before the Eternal One: harps, lyres and tambourines as well as timbrels and cymbals. And they had travelled as far as the threshing floor of Nachon, when the oxen stumbled and Uzzah put out his hand and grabbed hold of the ark. And the Eternal One was angry with Uzzah and God struck him down there because of his error, and Uzzah died there alongside the Ark of God.

2 Samuel 6:1-7

* * * * * * * * * * * *

TYPES OF PRAYER[40]

Decide whether you think these prayers are prayers of petition, gratitude, doxology or penitence (please, thanks, wow or oops!)

1) 'Who is like You, Eternal One, among the gods people worship? Who is like You, glorious in holiness, awesome in splendour, doing wonders?'

(Ge-ulah section, after the *Sh'ma* p.139)

2) 'Forgive us, our Creator, for we have sinned; pardon us, our Sovereign, for we have transgressed …'

(Weekday *Amidah*, p.55)

3) 'We give thanks that You, Eternal One, are our God, as You were the God of our ancestors.'

(Amidah, p.144)

4) 'Grant peace, welfare and blessing, grace love and mercy, to us and to all Israel, Your people.'

(ibid)

5) 'Praised be Your name, Eternal God, in heaven and on earth …'

(Yishtabbach, p.135)

6) 'Unending love have You shown Your people, the House of Israel …'

(Blessing preceding *Sh'ma*, p.93)

7) 'And now let us extol the Eternal God from this time and forever. Halleluyah!'

(p.111)

8) 'Bless this year for us, Eternal God: may its produce bring us well-being.'

(Weekday *Amidah*, p.56)

9) 'So long as there is a soul within me, I will give thanks to You, Eternal One, my God and God of my ancestors …'

(p.113)

10) 'Praise the One to whom our praise is due.'

(Bar'chu, p.135)

---

[40] Page references are from Liberal Judaism's prayerbook, *Siddur Lev Chadash*, ULPS, London 1995

LESSON NINE

'Thou shalt not'

Aims:
- To consider the need for guidelines and laws to regulate human behaviour.
- To consider the means and authority by which such laws might be enforced.
- To consider the difference between laws that are limited to a particular society and those that are relevant in all times and places.
- To emphasise that particular laws were introduced to answer specific questions or problems and that the task of a Liberal Judaism is to seek out what was the question to which a particular biblical law was the answer.

Objectives (ATEOTTCWBAT)
- Articulate an awareness of the need for rules at several levels of human existence.
- Articulate an awareness of the transient nature of some laws (especially biblical) and the permanence of others.
- Show an understanding that laws were introduced to answer or deal with particular questions and of the importance of seeking out the questions.
- Demonstrate an understanding of how laws need to be enforceable in order to be effective and the ways in which this is achieved in different societies.

Methodology:
Analysis of various laws from the Torah, some of which still have a place in our modern world, others that are clearly limited to the biblical environment that produced them. Use the five questions as a basis for focusing thoughts on relevance of laws to modern society – perhaps divide students into groups and have them report back. Focus the discussion on considering why such laws were necessary and what they were trying to achieve when they were introduced. *(Show and discuss Monty Python's 'Life of Brian*[41]*' stoning sketch to demonstrate folly of rigid application of laws.)*

0.00 – 0.40	Read biblical laws one at a time and ask participants to consider what situation in ancient Israel required the introduction of such a law, what was its purpose and is it still relevant today?
0.40 – 0.50	Discuss the need to apply laws with flexibility and that so many of the laws in the Torah are unworkable in our modern world. Emphasise that the important thing is to understand the purpose of the law rather than its 'correctness'.

Resources:
List of biblical laws for discussion (see below) and/or copies of *Tanakh*.
(DVD player or laptop computer.
Monty Python's 'Life of Brian'.)

---

[41] 'Monty Python's Life of Brian' (1979) directed by Terry Jones, DVD Sony Home Entertainment 2003.

BIBLICAL VERSES

Consider each of these laws and ask yourselves the following questions:

1) What situation existed that led to this law being introduced?
2) In what way did the law seek to address that situation?
3) What were the likely consequences of the law?
4) How successful do you think the law was?
5) Would the law work or is it still relevant today?

1.   'Six days may work be done but the seventh day shall be a Sabbath of complete rest, holy to the Eternal One; whoever does work on the Sabbath day shall be put to death.' (Exodus 31:15)

2.   'You shall not murder.' (Exodus 20:13)

3.   'When you reap the harvest of your land, you shall not reap all the way to the edges of your field, nor gather the gleanings of your harvest. You shall not strip your vineyard bare nor gather the fallen grapes; you shall leave them for the poor and the stranger: I the Eternal One am your God.' Leviticus 19:9-10)

4.   'You shall not boil a kid in its mother's milk.' (Exodus 23:19)

5.   'All winged swarming things that walk on fours shall be an abomination for you. But these you may eat among the winged swarming things that walk on fours: all those that have, above their feet, jointed legs to leap with on the ground. Of these you may eat the following: locusts of every kind; all kinds of bald locust, crickets of every kind; and all types of grasshopper. But all other winged swarming things that have four legs shall be an abomination for you.' (Leviticus 11:20-23)

6.   'There shall be an area for you outside the camp where you may relieve yourself. Included in your gear you shall have a spike, and when you have squatted you shall dig a hole with it and cover up your excrement. For the Eternal One your God moves about in your camp to protect you and to deliver your enemies to you; let your camp be holy; do not let God not find anything unseemly among you and turn away from you.' (Deuteronomy 23:13-15)

7.   'If a man has a stubborn and rebellious son who does not heed his father or mother and does not obey them even after they discipline him, his father and mother shall take hold of him and bring him out to the elders of his town at the public place of his community. They shall say to the elders of his town, "This son of ours is stubborn and rebellious; he does not heed us. He is a glutton and a drunkard." Thereupon the men of his town shall stone him to death.' (Deuteronomy 21:18-21)

8.   'When a woman has her regular flow of blood, the impurity of her monthly period will last seven days, and anyone who touches her will be unclean till evening. Anything she lies on during her period will be unclean, and anything she sits on will be unclean. When a woman has a discharge of blood for many days at a time other than her monthly period or has a discharge that continues beyond her period, she will be unclean as long as she has the discharge, just as in the days of her period.' (Leviticus 15:19-20,25)

9.   'Love your neighbour as you love yourself: I am the Eternal One' (Leviticus 19:18)

The following, which can be found on a number of public websites,[42] is included as a possible extra discussion item to focus on the question of literal adherence to biblical laws.

Dear Dr. Laura,

Thank you for doing so much to educate people regarding God's Law. I have learned a great deal from your show, and I try to share that knowledge with as many people as I can. When someone tries to defend the homosexual lifestyle, for example, I simply remind him that Leviticus 18:22 clearly states it to be an abomination. End of debate.

I do need some advice from you, however, regarding some of the specific laws and how to best follow them.

a) When I burn a bull on the altar as a sacrifice, I know it creates a pleasing odour for the Lord (Lev 1:9). The problem is my neighbours. They claim the odour is not pleasing to them. Should I smite them?

b) I would like to sell my daughter into slavery, as sanctioned in Exodus 21:7. In this day and age, what do you think would be a fair price for her?

c) I know that I am allowed no contact with a woman while she is in her period of menstrual uncleanliness (Lev 15:19-24). The problem is, how do I tell? I have tried asking, but most women take offence.

d) Lev. 25:44 states that I may indeed possess slaves, both male and female, provided they are purchased from neighbouring nations. A friend of mine claims that this applies to Mexicans, but not Canadians. Can you clarify? Why can't I own Canadians?

e) I have a neighbour who insists on working on the Sabbath. Exodus 35:2 clearly states he should be put to death. Am I morally obligated to kill him myself?

f) A friend of mine feels that even though eating shellfish is an Abomination (Lev 11:10), it is a lesser abomination than homosexuality. I don't agree. Can you settle this?

g) Lev 21:20 states that I may not approach the altar of God if I have a defect in my sight. I have to admit that I wear reading glasses. Does my vision have to be 20/20, or is there some room for manoeuvre here?

h) Most of my male friends get their hair trimmed, including the hair around their temples, even though this is expressly forbidden by Lev 19:27. How should they die?

i) I know from Lev 11:6-8 that touching the skin of a dead pig makes me unclean, but may I still play football if I wear gloves?

j) My uncle has a farm. He violates Lev 19:19 by planting two different crops in the same field, as does his wife by wearing garments made of two different kinds of thread (cotton/polyester blend). He also tends to curse and blaspheme a lot. Is it really necessary that we go to all the trouble of getting the whole town together to stone them? (Lev 24:10-16) Couldn't we just burn them to death at a private family affair like we do with people who sleep with their in-laws? (Lev. 20:14)

I know you have studied these things extensively, so I am confident you can help. Thank you again for reminding us that God's word is eternal and unchanging.

---

[42] e.g. http://www-users.cs.york.ac.uk/susan/joke/laura.htm

LESSON TEN

'Never mind the bullocks...'

Aims:
- To outline the history of ancient Israel under the rule of Judges and Kings up to the destruction of Israel in 722 BCE.
- To discuss the nature of tribal gods in that society.
- To consider the place and role of prophets in that society.

Objectives (ATEOTTCWBAT)
- Articulate an awareness of the history of ancient Israel and Judah based on the books of Judges, Samuel and Kings.
- Demonstrate some knowledge of the key figures, events and dates in the history of ancient Israel and Judah.
- Articulate an understanding of the role of key prophets: Hosea, Amos, Isaiah.

Methodology:
Run through Israelite history: brief stories of some of the antics of the Judges. (Information not included here but readily available). Explain how the Israelites wanted a king to bring them all together: Saul failed, David succeeded. Division of the kingdoms – use map to show relative size and location of Israel, Judah and their neighbours. Role of a kingdom's 'god' in battle – explain the perception and consequences of defeat. Introduce 'bullying' activity by asking children of their experiences of being bullied (or bullying), then relate this to the position of Israel and Judah vis-à-vis Assyria and Egypt. Divide into groups and get each group to set out its needs (Israel/Judah) or demands (Egypt/Assyria). More history: Israel is destroyed – does this mean that Israel's God has failed? (*Show prophets excerpt from 'Life of Brian'*[43].) Explain how the prophets made destruction the people's fault, not God's. Get students to read out speeches – dramatically! Emphasise the prophets' insistence that destruction was the people's fault for failing to do God's will in establishing justice.

0.00 – 0.25	Judges and Kings – summarise the history of the Israelites in Canaan using timeline, Judges' stories, maps.
0.25 – 0.35	Bullying: ask participants about bullying. Then divide into groups: empires (Assyria/Egypt) and vassals (Israel/Judah). Set out and discuss needs and demands.
0.35 – 0.50	Explain the destruction of Israel and consequences. Bring on the prophets – (*show brief excerpt from 'Life of Brian')'*, read speeches by Isaiah and Amos.

Resources:
Notes showing maps and highlights of ancient Israelite history.
(*Monty Python's 'Life of Brian' and laptop.*)
Prophetic speeches (attached)

---

[43] 'Monty Python's Life of Brian' (1979) directed by Terry Jones, DVD Sony Home Entertainment 2003.

MAPS

The locations of the twelve tribes of Israel	The kingdoms of Israel and Judah and their neighbours

Map showing extent of Assyrian and Babylonian Empires

• • • • • • • • • Assyrian Empire   – – – – – – – – – Babylonian Empire

HIGHLIGHTS OF ANCIENT ISRAELITE HISTORY

DATE	SIGNIFICANT CHARACTERS/EVENTS
1900 BCE 1800 BCE	Abraham & Sarah, Isaac & Rebekah, Jacob Rachel & Leah Joseph and his brothers The time of the patriarchs and matriarchs
1700 BCE	
1600 BCE	Israelites in Egypt (?)
1500 BCE	
1400 BCE	
1300 BCE	c 1350 Exodus from Egypt (?)
1200 BCE	The period of the Judges: Deborah, Ehud, Gideon, Jephthah etc
1100 BCE	The arrival of the Philistines: Samson
1000 BCE	Samuel the prophet at Shiloh, Saul becomes king, then David. David establishes Jerusalem as capital c 930 Solomon becomes king; builds Temple 922 Solomon dies, Israel and Judah split into 2 kingdoms Shishak of Egypt attacks Jerusalem
900 BCE	Elijah prophesies in Israel
800 BCE	Amos and Hosea prophesy in Israel, Isaiah and Micah in Judah 736 Israel and Syria attack Judah 727 Hezekiah becomes king of Judah 722 Assyria destroys Israel 701 Assyrian army besieges Jerusalem but withdraws.
700 BCE	Babylonians defeat Assyrians c 609 Jeremiah prophesies in Judah
600 BCE	597 Babylonians besiege Jerusalem 586 Jerusalem and Temple destroyed by Babylonians Judahites taken into exile

THE PROPHETS

Hear the word of the Eternal One, you rulers of Sodom;
listen to the law of our God, you people of Gomorrah!
"To what purpose is the multitude of your sacrifices unto Me?
says the Eternal One.
"I have had My fill of burnt offerings, of rams and the fat of fattened animals;
I have no pleasure in the blood of bullocks and lambs and goats.
When you come to appear before me, who has asked this of you,
 this trampling of my courts? Stop bringing meaningless offerings!
Your incense is detestable to me. New Moons, Sabbaths and gatherings—
I cannot abide your evil assemblies.
My soul hates your New Moon festivals and your appointed feasts.
They have become a burden to me; I am weary of them.
When you spread out your hands in prayer, I will hide my eyes from you;
even if you offer many prayers, I will not listen.
Your hands are full of blood; wash and make yourselves clean.
Take your evil deeds out of my sight!
Stop doing wrong, learn to do right!
Seek justice, support the oppressed.
Defend the orphan, plead the case of the widow."

Isaiah 1:10-17

Hear this, you who trample the needy and exploit the poor of the land, saying, "When will the New Moon be over that we may sell grain, and the Sabbath be ended that we may market our wheat?"
Making the *ephah* small, and the *shekel* great and cheating with dishonest scales, buying the poor for silver and the needy for a pair of sandals, selling even the discarded scraps with the wheat.
The Eternal One has sworn by the Pride of Jacob: "I will never forget anything they have done."

Amos 8:4-7

"I hate, I despise your religious feasts;
I cannot stand your assemblies.
When you bring Me burnt offerings and grain offerings, I will not accept them.
Though you bring choice meal offerings,
I will take no notice of them.
Away with the noise of your songs!
I will not listen to the music of your harps.
But let justice roll down like water,
righteousness like an ever-flowing stream!"

Amos 5:21-24

Hear this word, you cows of Bashan on Mount Samaria, you women who oppress the poor and crush the needy and say to your husbands, "Bring us some drinks!" The Eternal One has sworn in holiness: "The time will surely come when you will be taken away with hooks, every last one of you with fishhooks. You will each be dragged out through holes in the broken walls, and taken away towards Mount Hermon," declares the Eternal One.

Amos 4:1-3

This is the word that came to Jeremiah from the Eternal One: 'Stand at the gate of the Eternal One's house and there proclaim this message: "Hear the word of the Eternal One, all you people of Judah who come through these gates to worship the Eternal One. 3 This is what the Eternal One, the God of Israel, says: "Reform your ways and your actions, and then I will let you live in this place." Do not trust in deceptive words and say, "This is the Temple of the Eternal One, the Temple of the Eternal One, the Temple of the Eternal One!" If you really change your ways and your actions and deal with each other justly, if you do not oppress the alien, the fatherless or the widow and do not shed innocent blood in this place, and if you do not follow other gods to your own harm, then I will let you live in this place, in the land I gave your forefathers for ever and ever. But look, you are trusting in deceptive words that are worthless. Will you steal and murder, commit adultery and perjury, burn incense to Baal and follow other gods you have not known, and then come and stand before me in this house, which bears my Name, and say, "We are safe"- safe to do all these detestable things? Has this house, which bears my Name, become a den of robbers to you? But I have been watching!" declares the Eternal One.'

Jeremiah 7:1-11

LESSON ELEVEN
'The Babylonians are coming!'

Aims:

- To describe the political situation in the Ancient Near East, with particular emphasis on the covenant relationship.
- To explain the conditions that led to the destruction of Jerusalem by the Babylonians in 586 BCE.
- To consider the role of Jeremiah and other prophets in gathering the archived material and sending it into exile to become the Torah.
- To emphasise the uniqueness of the book of Deuteronomy.
- To consider the survival of the religion of Judah in Babylonian exile and its return to Jerusalem.

Objectives (ATEOTTCWBAT)

- Articulate an awareness of destruction of Jerusalem and the Temple and its implications for the people of Judah.
- Express an understanding of the importance of the people of Judah maintaining their identity in exile.
- Demonstrate recognition of the process of collation and editing that led to the production of the Five Books of Moses and the unique status of Deuteronomy.

Methodology:

(Begin by showing clips from the DVD 'Jeremiah[44]' depicting the destruction of Jerusalem and the Temple). (Alternative: present history of Babylonian siege of Jerusalem). Discuss the Babylonian practice of transplanting key figures to destroy local identity. *(Play Don McLean's 'By the Waters of Babylon'.[45])* Read Psalm 137 – discuss the desire to maintain identity and ways of doing so. Brainstorm contents of Torah (perhaps supply some supplementary material if the students' knowledge is not too sound), writing contents on flipchart. Discuss organisation of material and editorial concerns. Conclude by skimming through Deuteronomy (summary attached) and discuss when it was written and for whom.

0.00 – 0.10	*(Show scenes of Jerusalem's destruction from 'Jeremiah')* or introduce history of First Temple destruction.
0.10 – 0.20	Discuss Babylonian policy of assimilating captives; *(play Don McLean's 'By the Waters of Babylon')*, read Psalm 137, discuss Judahites' resistance.
0.20 – 0.35	Brainstorm contents of Torah (suggested list of contents attached).
0.35 – 0.40	Skim through contents of Deuteronomy.
0.40 – 0.50	Summarise compilation and composition of the Torah and its purpose: to give the exiled people of Judah their identity and connection to the land – and their return to it.

Resources: *(Laptop computer or DVD player.*
DVD of 'Jeremiah'.
Music of 'Babylon' – Don MacLean.)
Deuteronomy chapter 28 (attached).
List of Torah highlights (attached).
Flipchart and pen.
Summary of Deuteronomy (attached).

---

[44] 'The Bible – Jeremiah' (DVD), directed by Harry Winer, Direct Holdings Holland B.V. 2005

[45] 'Babylon' Don McLean 'American Pie' (CD) EMI, original recording 1971

Deuteronomy chapter 28

1 If you will promise to listen to the voice of the Eternal One your God and carefully observe all the commandments that I am giving you today, the Eternal One your God will set you high above all the nations of the earth. 2 All these blessings will come upon you and be with you if you listen to the voice of the Eternal One your God: 3 You will be blessed in the city and blessed in the country. 4 The fruit of your womb will be blessed, as will the crops of your field and the young of your livestock— the calves of your herds and the lambs of your flocks. 5 Your basket and your kneading trough will be blessed. 6 You will be blessed when you come in and blessed when you go out.

7 The Eternal One will ensure that enemies who rise up against you will be defeated. They will come at you from one direction but run away from you in seven. 8 The Eternal One will send a blessing on your barns and on everything you put your hand to. The Eternal One your God will bless you in the land you are being given. 9 The Eternal One will establish you as a holy people, as you were promised on oath, if you keep the commandments of the Eternal One your God and walk in God's ways. 10 Then all the peoples on earth will see that you are called by the name of the Eternal One, and they will fear you. 11 The Eternal One will grant you abundant prosperity— in the fruit of your womb, the young of your livestock and the crops of your ground— in the land God swore to your ancestors to give you. 12 The Eternal One will open the heavens, the storehouse of bounty, to send rain on your land in season and to bless all the work of your hands. You will lend to many nations but will borrow from none. 13 The Eternal One will make you the head, not the tail. If you observe the commandments of the Eternal One your God that I give you this day and carefully follow them, you will always be at the top, never at the bottom. 14 Do not turn aside from any of the commands I give you today, to the right or to the left; do not follow other gods or serve them.

15 However, if you do not promise to listen to the voice of the Eternal One your God and carefully observe all the commandments that I am giving you today, all these curses will come upon you and overtake you:

16 You will be cursed in the city and cursed in the country. 17 Your basket and your kneading trough will be cursed. 18 The fruit of your womb will be cursed, as will the crops of your land, and the calves of your herds and the lambs of your flocks. 19 You will be cursed when you come in and cursed when you go out. 20 The Eternal One will send you curses, confusion and rebuke in everything you put your hand to, until you are destroyed and come to total ruin because of the evil you have done in forsaking God. 21 The Eternal One will plague you with diseases until you have been destroyed from the land you are entering to possess. 22 The Eternal One will strike you with wasting disease, with fever and inflammation, with scorching heat and drought, with blight and mildew, which will plague you until you die. 23 The sky over your head will be like bronze, the ground beneath you like iron. 24 The Eternal One will turn the rain of your land into dust and powder; it will fall from the skies until you are destroyed. 25 The Eternal One will cause you to be defeated by your enemies. You will come at them from one direction but flee from them in seven, and you will become a thing of horror to all the kingdoms on earth. 26 Your carcasses will be food for all the birds of the air and the beasts of the earth, and there will be no one to frighten them away. 27 The Eternal One will afflict you with the boils of Egypt and with tumours, sores and the itching disease which cannot be cured. 28 The Eternal One will afflict you with madness, blindness and confusion. 29 At midday you will grope about in darkness like the blind. You will be unsuccessful in everything you do; you will be oppressed and robbed all your days, with no one to rescue you. 30 You will be betrothed to a woman, but another will take her and ravish her. You will build a house, but you will not live in it. You will plant a vineyard, but you will not even begin to enjoy its grapes. 31 Your ox will be slaughtered before your eyes, but you will not eat any of it. Your donkey will be forcibly taken from you and will not be returned. Your sheep will be given to your enemies, and no one will rescue them. 32 Your sons and daughters will be given to another nation, and you will wear out your eyes looking out for them day after day, incapable of lifting a hand. 33 Everything that you have worked to take from your land will be eaten by a people that you do not know and you will have nothing but cruel oppression for all time. 34 The things you see will drive you mad.

35 The Eternal One will afflict your knees and legs with painful boils that cannot be cured, spreading from the soles of your feet to the top of your head. 36 The Eternal One will drive you and the king

you set over yourselves to a nation unknown to you or your ancestors. There you will worship other gods, gods of wood and stone. 37 You will become a thing of horror and an object of scorn and ridicule to all the nations where the Eternal One will drive you. 38 You will sow much seed in the field but you will harvest little, because locusts will devour it. 39 You will plant vineyards and cultivate them but you will not drink the wine or gather the grapes, because worms will eat them. 40 You will have olive trees throughout your country but you will not use the oil, because the olives will fall off. 41 You will have sons and daughters but you will not keep them, because they will go into captivity. 42 Swarms of locusts will take over all your trees and the crops of your land. 43 The stranger who lives among you will rise above you higher and higher, but you will sink lower and lower. 44 He will lend to you, but you will not lend to him. He will be the head, but you will be the tail. 45 All these curses will come upon you. They will pursue you and overtake you until you are destroyed, because you did not obey the Eternal One your God and observe the commandments and decrees that God gave you. 46 They will be a sign and a wonder to you and your descendants for ever.

47 Because you did not serve the Eternal One your God joyfully and gladly in the time of prosperity, 48 therefore you will serve the enemies the Eternal One sends against you in hunger and thirst, in nakedness and dire poverty. God will put an iron yoke on your neck until you are destroyed. 49 The Eternal One will bring a nation against you from far away, from the ends of the earth, like an eagle swooping down, a nation whose language you will not understand, 50 a ruthless nation with no respect for the old or pity for the young. 51 They will devour the young of your livestock and the crops of your land until you are destroyed. They will leave you no grain, new wine or oil, nor any calves of your herds or lambs of your flocks until you are ruined. 52 They will lay siege to all the cities throughout your land until the mighty city walls in which you have trusted fall down. They will besiege all the cities throughout the land the Eternal One your God is giving you. 53 Because of the suffering that your enemy will inflict on you during the siege, you will eat the fruit of the womb, the flesh of the sons and daughters the Eternal One your God has given you. 54 Even the most gentle and sensitive man among you will have no compassion on his own brother or the wife he loves or his children, 55 and he will not give to one of them any of the flesh of his children that he is eating. It will be all he has left because of the suffering that your enemy will inflict on you during the siege of all your cities. 56 The most gentle and sensitive woman among you— so sensitive and gentle that she would not venture to touch the ground with the sole of her foot — will begrudge the husband she loves and her own son or daughter 57 the afterbirth from her womb and the children she bears. For she will eat them secretly during the siege and in the distress that your enemy will inflict on you in your cities. 58 If you do not promise to observe all the words of this teaching, which are written in this book, and do not revere this glorious and awesome name — the Eternal One your God— 59 the Eternal One will send fearful plagues on you and your descendants, harsh and prolonged disasters, and severe and lingering illnesses. 60 God will bring upon you all the diseases of Egypt that you dreaded, and they will cling to you. 61 The Eternal One will also bring on you every kind of sickness and disaster not recorded in this Torah, until you are destroyed.

62 You who were as numerous as the stars in the sky will be left but few in number, because you did not obey the Eternal One your God. 63 Just as it pleased the Eternal One to make you prosper and increase in number, so it will please God to ruin and destroy you. You will be uprooted from the land you are entering to possess. 64 The Eternal One will scatter you among all nations, from one end of the earth to the other. There you will worship other gods— gods of wood and stone, which neither you nor your ancestors have known. 65 Among those nations you will find no respite, no resting place for your feet. There the Eternal One will give you an anxious mind, eyes weary with longing, and a despairing heart. 66 You will live in constant tension, filled with dread both night and day, never sure of your life. 67 In the morning you will say, 'If only it were evening!' and in the evening, 'If only it were morning!' — because of the terror that will fill your hearts and the things that your eyes will see. 68 The Eternal One will send you back in ships to Egypt on a journey I said you should never make again. There you will offer yourselves for sale to your enemies as male and female slaves, but no one will buy you.

69 These are the terms of the covenant the Eternal One commanded Moses to make with the Israelites in Moab, in addition to the covenant God had made with them at Horeb.

TORAH HIGHLIGHTS

(Note: this is not an exhaustive list – elements in **bold** have been specifically mentioned in this course; others can be added based on students' or teacher's knowledge!)

Creation of the world – Adam and Eve – Cain and Abel – **Noah and the flood** – Tower of Babel – **Abraham and Sarah** – **Isaac and Rebecca** – Jacob and Esau – Jacob Leah and Rachel – Joseph and his brothers – **Twelve tribes go to Egypt** – Slavery – **Moses** – **Burning bush** – **10 plagues** – **Exodus** – **Mount Sinai** – Ten Commandments – Building the ark and the sanctuary – Golden Calf **Priestly laws (eg sacrifice, costumes, dietary regulations, illness, blood, Holiness Code,** *Pesach, Shavu'ot, Rosh ha-Shanah, Yom Kippur, Sukkot***)** – Journey through the wilderness – Ten Spies – Forty years – Arrival at borders of Promised Land –– **Laws** – covenant – consequences – Moses' farewell – death of Moses.

SUMMARY OF DEUTERONOMY

- Moses reviews the Israelites' travels from Egypt to the borders of the Promised Land, reminding the Israelites of what occurred at Mount Horeb (Sinai). (1:6 – 4:40)
- (4:44-26 end) Religious foundations of the covenant; Code of laws worship (12:1-16:17), government (16:18-18 end), criminal law (19:1-21:9), domestic life (21:10-25 end) sanctuary (26)
- 27-30 Covenant: enforcement of law, reinforcement of covenant
- 31-34: Last days of Moses

* * ** * * * * * * * *

SUGGESTED FURTHER READING

The following does not represent an exhaustive reading list; just some suggestions for those who would like to widen their perspectives on the origins of the Torah and many of the stories in it.

Blenkinsopp, Joseph, 'A History of Prophecy in Israel', The Westminster Press, Philadelphia, 1983

Friedmann, Richard Elliott, 'Who Wrote the Bible?', Harper Books, San Francisco 1997.

Goldberg, D.J. & Rayner J.D., 'The Jewish People' Penguin Books, London, 1987.

Kushner, Harold, 'To Life', Warner Books, New York, 1993.

Miller, J Maxwell & Hayes, John H., 'A History of Ancient Israel and Judah,' Westminster John Knox Press, Louisville, 1986.

Sperling, S.David, 'The Original Torah', New York University Press, New York 1998.

Tobias, Pete, 'Liberal Judaism: A Judaism for the Twenty-First Century', Liberal Judaism, London 2007

Wilson, Ian, 'The Bible is History', Weidenfeld & Nicolson, London 1999.

Wilson, Ian, 'The Exodus Enigma', Weidenfeld & Nicolson, London 1985.

www.liberaljudaism.org